Morgan James
Speakers Group

↗ www.TheMorganJamesSpeakersGroup.com

We connect Morgan James published
authors with live and online events
and audiences who will benefit
from their expertise.

D0709266

I'll probably get a crummy seat and feel squished for the entire flight. I'll miss seeing my daughter ride at the horse show. I hate missing my kids' activities. And, worst of all, I'll be in Newark for two days.

This string of thoughts occupied my mind for several hours, during which I made myself steadily more miserable.

Then I got to work and looked at my e-mail. A note sent the day before informed me that the hearing in Newark had been cancelled, so I didn't have to go.

All of that morning's unpleasantness—my worry, fear, and resistance—was completely unnecessary. And it was all caused by my thoughts—and *only* my thoughts.

Furthermore, those thoughts were completely untrue, even while I was thinking them. I spent hours worrying about a trip that had already been cancelled. For those hours, I lived in an unpleasant and totally self-created mental world.

We are often victims of our own thoughts. We automatically assume those thoughts are true, when in fact they often are not. As a result, we fill our lives with unpleasant mind states. Think how different my morning would have been if I hadn't focused my thoughts on my imaginary trip to Newark.

But we are not stuck with whatever thoughts arise. We can change them.

In the chapters to come, I'll show you just how this can be done.

3

Thinking is Overrated

Observing our mind's antics at close quarters and in real time, we discover we have a lunatic in the attic.
—David Michie

Most people believe that thinking is the only thing the mind does. But it can also do something that's fundamentally different, far more powerful, and far more capable of furthering our happiness:

It can be aware.

This is a capacity most of us rarely use.

In fact, thinking is vastly overrated. Our overuse of it creates much of our unhappiness.

Thinking has its place. Used properly, it can help us in many ways and many situations. But, too often, we revert to thinking when what we actually need to do is be aware.

Thinking causes the familiar, yammering voice in our heads that often spouts falsehoods, like mine did with my imaginary trip to Newark. But many of the falsehoods that arise from our thinking are far bigger, longer lasting, and more damaging than my imaginary trip. That voice can dominate our life—obsessing about an upcoming test, or a job interview, or whether we will be able to pay the rent.

Almost no one talks about this voice, or where it comes from, but we all have it. It's there late at night when you're trying to fall asleep. It can be your more-or-less constant companion during the day, commenting on everything. *Damn, I should have studied harder for that test. I should have started sooner, too. Jeez, I'm such a screw-off. I'll make up for it by studying hard this weekend. But, wait a minute, I have horseback riding. And I have to go to Mary's house. She'll be mad if I don't show up…*

One common name for this voice is the "inner critic," because it often compares us to others (usually unfavorably), or compares our performance against our goals, or focuses on a perceived fault or limitation.

This voice can easily make us miserable, if we let it. And it can make us miserable repeatedly if we give it a pattern to follow or a story to tell.

Actually, most of us have multiple conflicting voices. Over time, one of them typically becomes dominant. Yet that particular voice may not promote our long-term happiness.

For example, suppose you decide to start working out twice a week. You have a clear plan and a clear intention, but your own thinking tells you things that get in your way. *I'll get to it next week. I have too much to do. It's too hard for me today.*

Over time, this voice can become a persistent mental fixture, telling you who you are and what you can or cannot do. *I'm not a workout person.* Or, *I'm too busy to go to the gym this week.* Or, *I'm an engineer, not a bodybuilder.* The voice tells you a story that you eventually accept as true—yet it may not be true at all.

These mental stories have a purpose: they give us a seemingly fixed identity in an uncertain, constantly changing, infinitely variable world. Often they serve as shortcuts for making decisions.

But these stories often are driven by beliefs about who we are and how we fit (or don't fit) in the universe. Most of these stories are the result of how we were brought up and what society (or our parents) told us about who we are and should be.

Many of these stories are just plain false. Or, if they were true in the past, they are not true today.

For example, for many years our commonly held story was that women were not as smart or as capable as men. As a result, outside of a handful of professions—nursing, teaching, secretarial work—women did not have a place in the world of work.

For centuries, our culture taught us this story, and most people—both men and women—told it to themselves and believed it. This story defined many generations of women: how they thought about themselves, how they acted, how happy they were, and how they related to the world. It was completely false, yet it limited women's lives as if it were true. The story became reality, simply because people believed it.

Here are some other, more personal examples:

As a child, I went to Catholic school, where the nuns taught me that if I did not get good grades, I was a less valuable person than someone who did well. Over the years, I assimilated this belief. I felt that I was a flawed, second-rate person if I disappointed authority figures like my parents or my teachers. This eventually became a core belief for me: *Do well in everything, or you will be unworthy and hurt other people.*

Now I know the true story: that it is wise for each of us to try our best, but that we are all worthy regardless of whether we achieve our goals or please people in authority.

Another example: when I was very small, the other kids in the neighborhood were older and better at sports than I was. They didn't want to play ball with me because, as they often told me, I was no good at any kind of game. Soon that became my own belief, a story I told myself, and a part of my own self-image.

Then I got to junior high, where I got to live out a different story. There I met different kids (my same age), as well as some coaches who believed I had potential as a player. With their help, I was able to challenge my internal story and beliefs about myself. In my last year of junior high school, I became a championship quarterback.

First I was limited by a false story; later, I was encouraged by a more positive and more accurate one.

Sadly, false stories can keep any of us from growing or achieving goals; sadder still, they can keep us from setting goals in the first place.

Each of us has hundreds of such stories in our heads. Some come from our culture; some come from the families that raised us. Many we made up ourselves, often without realizing it. Virtually all of these stories spring from our core beliefs, and many of those beliefs simply don't reflect reality.

Each of us lives our life as a complex of these stories—the fat, unathletic kid; the artist who is no good at math; the thoughtful, quiet introvert; the devoted parent; the eccentric but big-hearted grandma. The list goes on and on. And most of us fall in love with our stories, even when they fail to serve us—and even when they are downright false.

Often people use their mental stories to justify their fears and inaction. These stories provide us with some comfort, and, often, a false sense that we needn't take responsibility for what we do. *I can't stop drinking this week; I'm too stressed out by work. I'm not smart enough to go to college. Looking for work is a waste of time with a job market this bad.* People use these stories to avoid acting and making choices, but their inaction only binds them further. (Whenever you start a sentence with "I can't"—or, more tellingly, "I should but I can't"—that's a clue that you are stuck in a mental story.)

As we've seen, the biggest problem with our mental stories is that they're often based on false beliefs. The second biggest problem is that we tend to repeat these stories to ourselves over and over, often perpetuating hopelessness, anger, depression, confusion, or imagined helplessness.

Thinking does not help in this situation. In fact, these stories are the direct result of our thinking. And we keep thinking and thinking and thinking—but, since we have already accepted the story, our thinking gets us nowhere. In fact, it moves us backward, by further perpetuating the story.

But there is good news—very good news. There is a way to loosen the grip of our mental stories, our false beliefs, and our incessant thinking.

This other way is fundamentally different from thinking. A key to happiness lies with developing this other capacity. And the really good news is that this other capacity already lies within us—we just need to awaken it.

4

Your Thoughts Are Not as Wise as You Are

n one important way, we're all like Superman, who can go into a telephone booth as Clark Kent, change clothes, and come out using a completely different set of powers.

Each of us can use a mental power that is completely different from thinking. This power can fundamentally change our experience of life and the way we interact with the world.

This power is awareness.

For now, think of awareness as the power to notice what is happening. This includes noticing your own thoughts and stories *without buying into them*, or becoming wrapped up in them.

Recognizing and cultivating awareness is central to happiness.

Awareness has the power to rewrite our mental stories. This is not always easy, but it is always possible. With practice, we can learn to observe our mental stories, see them for what they are, and let the inaccurate ones drop away.

We can also examine the beliefs underlying our stories to see how true they are. When we discover that a belief is untrue, we can change it. And once a belief changes, the stories that spring from it—and the things our inner voice says to us—will change as well.

As part of the process, we can also recognize the mental habits that do not lead to our genuine happiness, and drop them.

This is the power of awareness. The power to get out of a story. To view it from a different vantage point. To see any false beliefs upon which the story is based, and to correct them. To see unskillful mental habits we have acquired, and to let them go.

Awareness is an innate capability we all have. Our culture doesn't cultivate it—or, in many contexts, even recognize it—but if we focus on it, we can develop it.

It's like playing a sport or riding a bike. You have to practice it to learn how to do it well. You can't just read about it or think about it.

Much of this book is about how to become skilled at awareness.

Here's a simple but powerful way to get started:

We all know what it is like to be in the present moment. When you pay full attention to a physical activity—like when you are climbing a hill on a bike, or focused on hitting a ball, or riding a horse—you are in the present moment. When you are fully engaged with an activity happening right now—like reading this sentence—you are also in the present moment. You are alive here and now.

But when you are in a mental story, you are not in the here and now. You are reliving the past or worrying about the future. You are imagining, not experiencing.

So, when you realize that you are stuck in a mental story, focus on the here and now instead. When you stay in the present moment, many of your mental stories will simply dissolve.

The more aware you are of how your stories control you and limit your freedom, the more power you have to rewrite them.

Better still, as you practice awareness, you will be able to let go of your mental stories altogether, and simply be fully present.

5

We Can't Control What Enters Our Head—But We Can Control What We Do With It

The price of greatness is responsibility over each of your thoughts.
—Winston Churchill

Most people believe that they control their thoughts.

Many of us think we *are* our thoughts. We imagine that we're the commander of a starship. Our thoughts are the crew on deck, and we are in the captain's chair like Captain Kirk, controlling them.

But actually our minds are not that way at all. *We* are not that way at all.

Don't believe me? Try this simple experiment, which takes only a couple of minutes:

Get a timer and set it for sixty seconds. Then find a quiet place—or create one right where you are: shut off your computer, your TV, and your phone. Sit down and get comfortable.

For the next minute, pay attention to your breath, and *only* your breath. Don't think about anything else. Just watch the breath coming and going in your body. You can focus on your nostrils, or your lungs, or your abdomen—it doesn't matter which.

Let go of all thoughts. Don't think about when you have to leave for work, or what you are going to wear, or your next meal, or what you are going to do later. If you are in control of your thoughts, this should be easy.

Please turn on the timer now and spend a minute just watching your breath.

How did you do?

If you're like almost everyone else who has tried this experiment, within a few seconds thoughts started appearing in your mind. By the time the timer went off a minute later, you probably had multiple thoughts—possibly dozens.

We can notice a couple of things about this.

One is that we are not our thoughts. Our thoughts happen, and we can observe them. But although the thoughts are happening in us, they are not really us. We are simply the place where our thoughts happen.

Second, we don't control our thoughts. We can't stop them from occurring. Nor do we control which ones appear.

Here's another way to describe this situation. We have a consciousness or awareness that is behind our thoughts, that operates underneath our thinking mind. Our mind is like a stage and our thoughts are like the actors on the stage. We get to experience the play, but we don't get to control the actors.

Here's yet another way to look at it. Thoughts are like waves on the ocean—they happen naturally, and we know they will be there, but we can't predict exactly what form they'll take, or when they will arrive, or how powerful they will be at any given moment.

Your mind is like your mouth. Mouths produce saliva—that is what mouths do. Your mind produces thoughts—that is what minds do. You cannot stop it or control it. You can try, but you won't succeed, and you'll probably get a headache.

And, of course, as we've already seen, our thoughts are not always true. In fact, they are often utterly false.

At this point you're probably thinking, "Wait a minute. Earlier you said that you can change your attitude and your thoughts, and this will make you happier and your life much better. But if you can't control your thoughts, then how in the world can you change them?"

It's a good question. But control is different from change. While we can't control exactly which thoughts show up in the first place, we *can* control which ones we pay attention to, and which ones we act on.

This is always your choice: which thoughts to honor, attend to, and act on, versus which ones to just let go. And when you just let go of a thought, it will dissipate, just as waves in the ocean do.

We all have this ability, this awareness. You just experienced it yourself when you spent a minute following (or trying to follow) your breath. You were aware of your breath, and then you became aware of your thoughts as they bubbled up.

Thoughts need to be fed in order to take center stage, and what they feed on is attention. When you are aware enough to place your attention where you want to place it, you can choose which thoughts will stay on the stage. If you don't give your attention to a thought, but simply observe its arrival without throwing yourself into it, it will dissipate, like a wave rolling onto a beach.

The more attention you give to a thought, the more it can grow and proliferate, or even temporarily take over your mind. You can get pulled into some magnificent stories in which you are the victim, or the perpetrator, or the success, or the failure, or the hero, or the villain.

None of us can control what thoughts come into our heads. But we are each responsible for which ones we pay attention to and give power to. In that way, we have the ability to change our thoughts.

As you practice simply observing the natural rise and fall of your thoughts, over time many troubling thoughts won't show up as strongly, or as often, or at all. If and when they do appear, they won't stay around long.

Through this simple act of observation, you will also get better at noting which thoughts are true and which ones are fantasies. In addition, you'll see for yourself how thinking is often overused and overrated.

With practice, you will also create the internal conditions that will make kindness and compassion show up more frequently—and hate, greed, and anxiety less often.

By the way, that act of simple observation—that one minute of following your breath, seeing your thoughts bubble up, and simply letting them go—has a name: meditation. Or, more specifically, mindfulness meditation.

6

Much of What We Believe is Wrong

Whether you think you can, or whether you think you can't, you're right.
—Henry Ford

f we cling to our thoughts or take them too seriously, they become beliefs—about our self, about the world, and about how we fit into it. These beliefs can control our experience of life.

Many of our beliefs do not reflect the way the world really is—or how *we* really are. Yet much of our stress and suffering arise from our beliefs. As a result, the less we cling to inaccurate beliefs, the less stress and suffering we experience. Often, the less stress and suffering we cause, as well.

False beliefs cause suffering in two related ways. First, if we believe things about the world that aren't true, we run into conflicts with reality, and this hurts. Second, if we believe things about *ourselves* that aren't true, we suffer for the same reason, but also because we limit our potential.

For example, the law of gravity is real. If you believed gravity didn't exist, it would put you in conflict with physical reality. You'd walk off a balcony and quickly come into conflict with the reality of gravity, as well as the reality of the hard ground below. This would be very painful for you. If you landed on someone else, it would also be terribly painful for them.

The same is true of a core belief that doesn't match up with other facets of reality. Sooner or later, that belief will put you in conflict with how things actually are, and that conflict will be painful.

One core belief most of us have is that happiness comes from the acquisition of things external to ourselves. That belief is false, and it causes a lot of suffering in people's lives. People endlessly search for happiness in things, and never find it. Instead they find *unhappiness*, because they have based their search on a false premise—in fact, on an impossibility.

We base much of our lives on such false beliefs. For example, we believe that the past automatically dictates the future. Or we believe that all fear is valid and appropriate. Or we believe that other people make us mad. None of these is true, and if we believe these ideas, eventually we will run into conflict with reality, and we will suffer.

It's easy to get trapped by false beliefs. They become glasses we put on every morning. They color our view of life and, thus, how we behave. They generate many of our thoughts, hopes, fears, and expectations, all of which can limit us. They are the source of our most troubling internal voices.

Many such beliefs were formed when we were young, by our upbringing, our culture, and our personal experiences. Back then, some of these beliefs may have been partly valid—or, at least, may have served a purpose—but even though they are inaccurate today, they remain with us.

In their book *Prisoners of Belief*, Matt McKay and Patrick Fanning offer a detailed look at how false core beliefs operate. In one example, McKay and Fanning compare two people who grew up during the 1960s in Harlem. Both people were equally smart and equally capable.

One of the people never got out of Harlem. She was bright and capable, but considered herself worthless, incapable, and victimized. She spent her entire life in poverty, blaming others for her situation.

The other was James Baldwin, who became one of the most important American writers of the twentieth century. From a young age, Baldwin believed in his own ability and intelligence. In high school, he was the literary editor of his school magazine. When he was 29, he published the bestselling novel *Go Tell It On the Mountain*.

The key difference between these people was what they believed about themselves and their world.

Now, it is true that talent has a lot to do with how far one goes—and Baldwin was an exceptionally talented writer. It's also true that circumstances can greatly impact how far even the most talented people go in the world. But Baldwin would have gone nowhere had he been trapped by the core belief that he was worthless, incapable, and victimized.

Another way to look at false beliefs is as activities of the mind that can be put to rest. They are the seeds of inaccurate thoughts, which we can let go of. Thus we can become free from the problems that these thoughts bring to our life.

As an example, imagine a man who does not believe he has anything to offer the world, who believes he is incompetent and will always fail. This man might have formed that belief at a young age because his parents, or siblings, or teachers repeatedly told him that.

Or maybe they didn't explicitly say this to him, but they always acted as if they expected him to fail.

Two things often happen for this unfortunate man. First, because he believes this message, he creates a set of internal rules for his conduct in life that accord with this belief. One of these rules is that he shouldn't try anything new, because he will fail. This keeps his life small and limited.

The second thing that happens is that an inner voice is informed by this false belief. When he has an opportunity to do or try something new, this inner voice says, *No way. I can't do that. It's beyond me.* The inner monologue makes this man feel miserable, over and over.

Another way to look at this is that these false beliefs are filters which shape our view of reality, like different colored sunglasses can color our view of everything we see. When we put them on, our perception of what is true, and what is possible, is colored, often in ways that lead to our unhappiness.

The truth, of course, is that everyone has value and abilities, and everyone is worthy of love and respect. We also all have limitations, and we all make mistakes. Sometimes we don't act as well as we'd like. But every one of us is already whole and complete.

We each have the power to identify the false beliefs that drive our inaccurate and painful inner stories. We can then let go of those beliefs and, instead, live in reality. We can be realistic in the truest sense of the word.

As you will see, this will naturally lead to a happier life.

The next few chapters look at some commonly held—but false—core beliefs.

7

The Belief That Happiness Comes from Getting What We Want is False

---

Joy does not come from what you do. It flows into what you do.
—B. Alan Wallace

O ne of most people's core beliefs is that our happiness depends on getting what we want—that the more the world conforms to our desires, the happier we will be.

A related belief is that our current situation is insufficient or inadequate, and that our internal resources are not enough to bring us happiness. According to this perspective, we need to acquire what will make us happy—and we need to do so endlessly.

These beliefs are dead wrong. Living our lives based on these untruths will regularly create conflicts with reality—and it will make us unhappy.

B. Alan Wallace calls this approach the *hunter-gatherer solution.* First we need to hunt down and acquire the things—the objects, relationships, and experiences—that will ostensibly make us happy. Then, once we've gathered them, we need to hold onto them tightly. And we need to constantly create plans for seeking, gathering, and keeping these things.

We can spend our lives on this hunt, acquiring a nice car, a good job, an attractive partner, obedient children who make us proud of them, and so on and on.

Behind this endless hunt is the sense that what we start with— what we have without these things—is insufficient.

This approach guarantees us unhappiness. It's not that there's anything wrong with a good car, a meaningful job, great kids, etc. The problem is with the hunter-gatherer mindset itself. That approach to happiness forces us to strive and strive and strive—and then, once we get something we want, to hold onto it for dear life. Once we have gotten something that we believe will make us happy, we want to keep it to keep ourselves happy. We also want it not to change, or diminish, or grow old. As a result, people who live according to the hunter-gatherer mindset spend a lot of their time fighting to keep what they have from changing or slipping away. Or trying to acquire new things when the previously acquired things do go away, or lose their allure.

For most of us, this approach takes up most or all of our conscious life.

It's exhausting, isn't it?

This approach fails in three ways:

First, we don't always get the things that we think will make us happy, no matter how hard we try.

Second, if we *are* lucky enough to get something we want, it doesn't keep us happy for long. The happiness disappears almost instantly, and we start on the next quest.

Third, things change. Sooner or later, we lose the very thing that we hunted, gathered, and acquired. The pie is all eaten. The puppy grows up. The new couch gets old and dirty. The perfect job becomes painful and difficult when our boss retires.

As a result, we end up afraid and anxious instead of happy. In fact, the hunter-gatherer approach is one of the reasons why anxiety, depression, and addiction are so rampant.

Yet, no matter how many things we acquire, and no matter how often this process fails us, most of us never change our attitude.

Fortunately, there is another approach—one that is based on what is true, not false.

You can start from an awareness that what you have right now inside you is sufficient for your happiness.

This does not mean you stand still and do nothing. But, instead of attempting to hunt and gather your way to happiness, you cultivate the internal capacities that already exist inside you. And you share them with those around you.

Think of a garden that's already been planted. If you cultivate it, it will grow into nourishing food or gorgeous flowers. In a similar way, by cultivating what is already within us, we can help our inner resources to develop and flourish.

This approach doesn't mean you won't find pleasure or fun, or that you won't be passionate about relationships, friends, work, or life in general. In fact, in practice it means precisely the opposite: you will experience *more* pleasure and fun, and become *more* passionate about your life. This is because you are bringing openness and energy to your life instead of banking on the hope that the things or situations you chase after will bring you what you yearn for.

In a life based on cultivation instead of hunting and gathering, there is much less anxiety and fear, because you know that your happiness doesn't depend on getting what you want, or keeping what you have.

Real happiness is achieved by transforming the mind, by changing how you approach life.

8

You Can Try to Pave Every Path, or You Can Make Some Shoes

Look at every path closely and deliberately, then ask ourselves this crucial question: Does this path have a heart? If it does, then the path is good. If it doesn't, it is of no use.
—Carlos Castaneda

ong ago, before the invention of shoes, there lived a very young prince. One day, as he walked on the paths outside his castle, he stubbed his toe on a root. This was very painful. His other foot came down hard on a rock, and that hurt as well.

He went to his father the king, complaining and crying in pain. His father ordered one of his high-ranking officials to have the army go around the entire kingdom and smooth out all the paths, taking out all the roots and removing all the rocks, so the prince would never again encounter pain as he walked.

The official was a wise man. He quickly realized it was an impossible task. There were thousands of miles of paths, and soon after the soldiers completed the task, more roots would grow and more rocks would roll onto the paths.

The official came up with an idea. He taught the prince how to take some leather, cut it perfectly, sew it into two protective structures, and put them on his feet. That way the prince could walk anywhere. There would still be roots and rocks to deal with, but the prince's shoes would enable him to limit difficulties and avoid pain.

In this story, the two approaches to protecting the prince's feet represent two different approaches to a happy life. Most of us have been taught that the way to happiness is to remove (or, sometimes, walk around) the roots and rocks that we encounter. As a result, we spend much of our time looking ahead, further down the path, trying to anticipate what roots and rocks may be there, and creating strategies for dealing with them, so that we won't be hurt by them.

This creates a more-or-less constant level of anxiety. Will we spot all the roots and rocks? Will we be able to remove them all, or at least walk around them? This strategy also makes us fixate on our memories of many of the roots and rocks we have stumbled over. In many cases, we also feel guilty about our mistakes and oversights.

Does this approach sound like it can lead to long-term happiness?

But there is also a fundamentally different approach. Instead of trying to change everything about the world, we can change ourselves by building our internal resources and abilities. We can then walk the path of life without great difficulty or pain—despite all the roots, rocks, and bumps we encounter.

Peace and happiness are available to us in every moment. They are within each of us. In fact, they are our natural state. There is no original sin—only original happiness. All we need to do is return to this natural state.

Lama Surya Das describes this state beautifully in his book *Awakening the Buddha Within*: "Completely comfortable and at ease in every situation—at peace in every circumstance, with a sense of true inner freedom independent of whatever outer circumstances or inner emotions present themselves."

Instead of trying to control the world and remaking it to our liking, we can turn our attention within. We can be responsible for our own happiness. We can let go of thoughts of control and ideas about victims and perpetrators, achievement and failure.

Most of us spend much of our time working on—and worrying about—the external events in life. But, as we've seen, our ability to control those events is very limited.

Instead, it's worth spending time—lots of time—training our mind.

This is a radical notion. It runs counter to how most of us live—racing through our day, checking our phones constantly, and worrying about the next thing we want to acquire, how we are going to acquire it, how we are going to keep what we have and avoid what we don't want, and how we are going to someday retire from this constant madness.

And it is indeed madness. We're running around, stubbing our toes left and right on rocks and roots, while telling ourselves we don't have time to make the shoes that would allow us to walk the path peacefully.

Building shoes is a radical change in priorities. With this approach, the most important item on your to-do list is to be fully present here and now. It means to bring your heart with you to every path you walk—regardless of the terrain you encounter.

This approach also requires that you spend some time each day working with your mind and heart, so that they aren't injured by the inevitable rocks and roots, sickness and death, and unfortunate and unwanted events that show up on your path. This frees you from having your happiness dictated by what happens (or doesn't happen) to you.

The rest of this book focuses on creating the shoes you can wear as you walk the path of life.

This way of living requires cultivation and patience. It involves bringing out qualities that have always been in you, but which you may have ignored or forgotten.

As you will see for yourself, everything you need to be happy is already within you.

This approach does not mean you will not be engaged with life. Indeed, it makes you *more* engaged and more willing to make a positive difference. It just means that your moment-to-moment peace will not depend on whether the path in front of you is free of rocks and roots.

As you will discover for yourself, this approach favors lightness, humor, and a not-so-serious attitude.

Peace and happiness are available to us in every moment. This means that every moment matters. Each moment—this moment— is unique and precious. It will never be replaced, and it will never happen again.

Each moment of life presents us with a mystery, a fabulous adventure. Why miss a moment of it by being anxious about whether it will happen according to the way you think you need it to be in order to be happy? Let it happen and enjoy the path.

9

The Truth Can Win Out—
If You Let It

You have always been and are now whole, complete, and sufficient. It is more fun to play the game of life from a perspective of sufficiency than deficiency—the price of admission is the same.
—David Gregson, Jay S. Efran, and G. Alan Marlatt
The Tao of Sobriety

Most of us believe that we suffer from a basic fault, that we are deficient or lacking in some fundamental way. The details are different for each person, but beneath these details is a belief that we need to achieve or perform in order to be loved—or even to *deserve* love. We feel we need to achieve in order to prove that we are valuable.

This is another very prevalent false belief, and it causes a great amount of suffering.

This belief requires us to achieve again and again—and, in the end, there will never be enough accomplishment. Michael Balint's brilliant book *The Basic Fault* examines this phenomenon beautifully and in detail.

As you will discover for yourself, none of this is true. In truth, we are all already whole, complete, and perfect just the way we are.

This perfection is unconditional. It doesn't depend on your actions or habits or performance or beliefs.

You can never prove to yourself that you are valuable, because it is not provable. You just *are*. It's like trying to prove that something is red. You can't prove it. It just is.

The problem is that most of us equate ourselves with our behaviors. We determine our value as human beings by judging our behaviors. And our behaviors are never perfect—after all, we are human.

But you are not your behaviors. Nor are you the things you have, or your skills or capacities, or the things you achieve (or don't achieve), or the roles you play in life (father, daughter, student, girlfriend, etc.).

Now, it's also true that each of us has acquired some behaviors that are not very skillful, and that we'd be better off without. So we'd be wise to let go of those unhelpful behaviors. But this is a very different thing from having some basic, intrinsic fault.

It's also true that each of us has limitations. I can't play basketball in the NBA. I don't have the physical skill, and I'm too old. I have not always been the best father, or student, and I constantly try to improve in those, and other roles I have. But those limitations don't make me deficient; they make me human.

Living life to the fullest, and developing and using our talents, has nothing to do with proving our value.

Accepting—or, if you prefer, believing in—our inherent value and perfection makes it easier to eliminate our unskillful behaviors.

It also helps us get rid of unhelpful roles—of victim, or perpetrator, or sinner, or saint.

The funny thing is that once you start seeing the world this way, you can accomplish more—sometimes a lot more. Here's something else: *what you choose to accomplish becomes easier.* And you are happier while you are accomplishing it.

This is the truth—and some say the secret—of life. And none of it needs to be proven. It just is. If you simply allow yourself to see it, it will be there right in front of you—and it will win out.

10

Pain is Unavoidable; Suffering is Optional

Pain is a relatively objective, physical phenomenon; suffering is our psychological resistance to what happens. Events may create physical pain, but they do not in themselves create suffering. Resistance creates suffering. Stress happens when your mind resists what is....The only problem in your life is your mind's resistance to life as it unfolds.

—Dan Millman

Pain is inevitable. It happens regularly. You stub your toe on the edge of the bed (maybe for the tenth time) and it hurts. You injure your knee skiing. You feel deep grief when you lose someone you love. You experience disappointment when someone else you love lets you down.

All of these are natural parts of human existence.

But pain is not the biggest problem in most people's lives. It's what we do with the pain.

Usually, we create a story around our pain. *I'm such a klutz.* Or, *The people who designed this bed are morons.* Or, *I was crazy to buy this damn bed. I need to get a new one.*

As we saw in Chapter 3, these stories are completely made up— and usually false. Sometimes they provide us with a small degree of temporary comfort. But mostly they cause us more pain.

Often our stories aren't specific to the situation. They're based on general (and often false) core beliefs. *I can't handle this.* Or, *Life is unfair.* Or, *I screwed up. It's my own damn fault.* Or, simply, *Poor me.* Or, perhaps most common of all, *My life sucks.*

We can think of pain and suffering as two arrows. A painful event is like getting nicked in the arm by a flying arrow. It hurts. But then we tell ourselves a story about the first arrow. This is like plunging a second arrow directly into our arm. This second arrow is usually far more painful than the first—and we're the one who wielded it.

A lot of this is caused by our having a false belief that we are entitled to a world without pain. We suffer because we tell ourselves that painful events shouldn't happen to us. Or, perhaps, that if only we are careful enough, or thorough enough, or if only we have the right attitude, or if we're good enough, then painful events will never happen to us. In short, we believe that painful events are somehow our fault.

These beliefs are entirely false—and they create considerable suffering. Yet most of us spend much of our time—and create much of our suffering—by shooting these arrows at ourselves.

Behind these arrows is a desire for the world to be different from the way it actually is.

But we do not have to live this way. We have choices in how we respond to any painful event.

One choice is to let our conditioned beliefs and stories take over, adding suffering to our pain.

Another choice is to try to ignore the pain, or run from it, or deny it, or tell ourselves that it isn't real, or that we shouldn't feel it. Paradoxically, these reactions only keep us stuck in our pain—for hours, days, or even years.

But we have a third choice. We can embrace the experience, including the pain that is part of it. Instead of running from the pain, or denying it, or resisting it, or writing a story about it—or about ourselves—we can simply accept it. We change our response from *I can't handle this!* to *What can I learn from this?* We can let go of *Life is unfair!* and embrace *How can this make me a better person?*

This takes focus and courage. It is not easy, but it is possible.

We can replace our false core beliefs about pain with a true belief—that it is part of life, but it is manageable. Or even that it is there for our benefit, because it will spur us to make changes which will actually make our life better.

I am *not* saying, "Don't be sad." I'm saying the opposite: *embrace your sadness,* and ask yourself, *What good can come of this? What can I learn from it?*

Pain is a powerful thing. We should not waste it. It can be transformative precisely *because* it is so powerful. Pain can serve us if we recognize it and accept it, without adding suffering to it.

When we do this, we are then free to investigate why it is there; to ask, *What can this teach me?;* and to change how we act or what we believe about the world.

When someone we love dies, we have a choice. We can play the victim and say to ourselves, *Why did they die so soon?* or *Why did God take them away from me?* Or we can use the pain of their death to teach us to treat each moment of our own life as precious.

When someone we care about lets us down, we can let the pain of our disappointment create a "poor me" story. Or we can let the pain teach us to look closely at our expectations, and to hold them more lightly.

Whenever we feel the arrow of pain, we always have a choice. We can try to hide from it inside a mental story, thereby adding suffering to our pain. Or we can learn from it; courageously use the pain to transform ourselves; and live a fuller life as a result.

Choosing courage will lead us to happiness.

11
Easy Isn't What it's Cracked Up to Be

All of us have had people tell us that their lives are hard. All of us have also told ourselves that *our own* lives are hard.

Most of us want our lives to be easy. We believe easy is better, so we try to hold on to easy and avoid hard.

Our culture promotes easy. We're taught that people are happy when they are comfortable, and unhappy when they are not.

This is all completely backward.

The quest for endless easy is a fool's errand. No one has a life that's always easy. Do you know a single person who has completely escaped sickness, or injury, or serious disappointment, or the death o

someone they cared about? If we're on a quest for a life of ease, we'll always fail, and always be unhappy.

Easy does not teach us much. It may be relaxing or fun. It may distract you from some of the painful parts of life. But easy won't help you learn about yourself and the world. It won't help you respond to challenges. It won't help you to create and live a bold vision.

Too much easy makes us soft and dull. We get used to easy, and we get spoiled. As a result, we stop trying new things and take fewer and fewer risks. Over time, what was easy becomes hard, and our life gets smaller and smaller.

In short, the pursuit of easy leads to suffering.

When you face something that you regard as hard, don't ask, *Why me?* Instead, ask, *What can I learn here? How can I use this for transformation?*

Life begins at the edge of your comfort zone and extends beyond it. Strange as it sounds, easy leads to suffering, but what's hard at first ultimately leads to happiness.

When easy comes, enjoy it. And when hard things come, enjoy them, too, by recognizing them as opportunities to expand your life and learn something new.

12

We Live in a Sea of Uncertainty—But We Already Know How to Swim

Security is mostly a superstition. It does not exist in nature, nor do the children experience it. Avoiding danger is no safer in the long run than outright exposure. Life is either a daring adventure, or nothing.
—Helen Keller

Uncertainty is a major cause of unhappiness in most people's lives. But it doesn't need to be.

Once we accept uncertainty, it creates hope, positive anticipation, creativity, and alertness. But if we refuse to accept it, it turns to fear. It's our choice.

We live in a sea of uncertainty, of not knowing what the future will bring. We also live in a world of impermanence, where everything changes and eventually disappears—including each of us.

Uncertainty and impermanence are all around us, all the time. They are unavoidable parts of the human condition.

Yet we bank our happiness on the false belief that things can somehow be made certain, or permanent, or within our control. This conflict between belief and reality leads to great unhappiness.

We can never be sure where each action we take will lead us (or others). And we can never be sure how long an experience we're enjoying will last.

Our life always contains uncertainty, but there are certain times when we notice it more—when we move, for example, or begin high school or college, or retire, or start a new job, or lose or leave our current one.

Our problem is not really with uncertainty or impermanence, however, but with how we handle them. This depends entirely on the attitude you bring to the uncertainty.

You are never more uncertain than when someone gives you an unexpected gift. There it is, all wrapped up, and you have no idea what it is. You are pleased, hopeful, and perhaps excited. You are also alert and awake—fully present. Maybe that's why we call gifts *presents*—they bring us into the present.

Uncertainty is not inherently a problem at all.

So, in those times when we have a problem with uncertainty, it's not because of the uncertainty itself, but the attitude we bring to it.

How would you feel if, in every moment, you were given an unexpected gift?

In fact, that is exactly what happens in life. In each new moment, the universe presents us with a new, unexpected gift.

Our problem is that we fool ourselves into thinking that many of the things we receive aren't gifts, but problems (or potential problems). But that is because we are conditioning our happiness on getting the thing we want, and not being open to what life brings us.

We already know how to approach life with excitement and anticipation. We do it every time we get that unexpected present, that compliment, or that hug.

But sometimes we forget to bring that same mindset to the new and unexpected event unfolding around us.

Starting now, you can begin to remember.

13

What We Do is Not as Important as How We Are

The mind can make a heaven out of hell
or a hell out of heaven.
—John Milton

Our culture focuses on doing—on making things happen and getting things done. As a result, many of us can be better described as *human doings* than *human beings*.

This is understandable, since one of the main beliefs ingrained in us by our culture is that happiness depends on going after and acquiring what we want. If we do X or Y, we will get A or B, and then, supposedly, be happy.

Yet, as we have already seen, this focus actually blocks the path to genuine happiness.

Here's a radically different concept: instead of focusing on *what* you *do*, focus on *how* you *are*—i.e., how you show up—in this moment.

This is important especially when you are not doing so well. When you are angry, or sad, or depressed, or bored, or anxious, or fearful, or guilty, or lonely, or ashamed, examine your mind. Watch as the emotions rise, twirl about, and perhaps grow or subside. Don't act on them, or try to embrace them, or try to push them away. Just watch them calmly, with compassion but without judgment.

When you are delighted, or joyous, or giddy, or energized, or deeply comfortable, treat those emotions in the same way. Don't try to hang onto them or get rid of them. Watch them and fully experience them.

Our "doing" culture teaches us not to examine our emotions. Instead, it tells us that when our emotions are painful, we should try to fix them, or escape from them, or deny them. Alternatively, we're taught to try to fix the people or events or situations that we imagine "make" us feel the way we do.

Sometimes changing the world—or other people—is easy and works just fine. We step under an awning and avoid the rain. We put plugs in our ears and sleep through the late-night party next door. We ask the person sitting behind us on the plane to have their kids stop kicking the back of our seat.

But altering the condition that is "causing" our pain isn't always possible. We can't make the grocery-store line shorter, or cause the stock market to rise instead of drop. And sometimes we can't stop the kids behind us from kicking the seat, even if we speak to them and their parents several times.

Often, *doing* simply isn't an option—or isn't going to help.

In these cases, you can simply be aware of your emotional state, without reacting to it or running from it. You can also ask yourself, *What is prompting this emotion?*

For example, in the case of the kids kicking the seat, the first answer might be *This is annoying—the plane should be a place of peace and quiet.* But that's not the real answer. After all, if you were sitting next to your best friend, the two of you might be loud and animated, and thus a bit disruptive.

Beneath the blame—and your annoyance—might be something like this: *I'm tired and I want to nap—but these kids are keeping me awake, so I'm frustrated.* Or it might be, *I'm trying to do this Sudoku, but these kids are distracting me, so doing the puzzle is more difficult and less fun. I'm disappointed.* Or it might be, *I'm pissed. Why can't these kids do as they are told?*

And beneath the frustration and disappointment and anger will be this: *I wish things would be different than they are right now.* Or this: *The world isn't living up to my expectations! It's not behaving the way I want it to—or the way I believe it should.*

Yet it's not the world that's out of sync, but your beliefs about it.

Your anger or frustration or disappointment is telling you something important—that you aren't living in accord with reality, with the here and now.

Once you see this, and understand what's prompting your pain, you can stop wrestling with reality. You can simply accept the situation—both the bother from the seat behind you and your own unpleasant emotions about it.

And at this point, something interesting may start to happen: those emotions may peak and then begin to subside.

Much of the time, the world simply won't operate in the exact way we want it to. This isn't a profound revelation. *You already know this; in fact, all of us do.* But few of us have learned to live by it.

You now have the opportunity to be one of those few.

No matter what is happening, you always have the power to examine your own emotions and the beliefs underlying them. Then you have the power to change the beliefs and let go of the emotions. This enables you to live in peace with the reality of the moment.

This doesn't mean giving up on what you believe is right, or on your passion for it. But it *does* mean that, even as you work for what is right and just, your happiness isn't based on how closely the universe conforms to your beliefs, hopes, and expectations.

You can't always change the world, or the people in it, in the way that you'd like. But you always *can* change your expectations or beliefs about whether your happiness is dictated by the situation the world presents to you.

14

"You Make Me Mad" is a Fantasy

Holding on to anger is like grasping a hot coal with the intent of throwing it at someone else; you are the one who gets burned.
—Buddha

When most of us get angry, we say that some event or person made us mad.

But that doesn't ring true. We're not mere anger machines who get mad whenever someone pushes the right button.

Instead, when we get angry, it's our own mind that creates the anger.

Imagine that you're driving down the highway with a good friend, having a pleasant conversation. Suddenly another driver cuts you off. You stop talking with your friend and shout, "Jerk! Don't you know how dangerous that is? Don't you know the basic rules of the road? There are other drivers on this highway, dammit!"

In only a few seconds, you raised your own blood pressure, impaired your ability to drive safely, disrupted your conversation with your friend, and made yourself miserable. Meanwhile, the driver who "made" you angry has gone on his merry way. You've grasped a hot coal and gotten burned.

You may also have perpetuated the habit of venting your anger at someone else whenever your expectations are not met. As a result, the next time reality falls short of your expectations, you'll be inclined to vent once again—this time at your spouse, or the child behind you in the airplane kicking your seat, or a co-worker. Another hot coal, and more burning.

Sometimes your anger may in fact change others' behavior to be what you want, at least temporarily. Some people may indulge you or give in to your demands just to avoid your wrath. But the damage this will create will ultimately lead to distrust and unhappiness. The people who do your bidding to avoid your anger will likely resent you, and may later push back, or seek revenge, or sabotage you.

Also, as we've seen, getting your way is not the key to either success or happiness.

In addition, anger never improves decision making. When we are angry, we are more likely to act in a way that will only promote more distress—that will toss more coals into a burning fire.

Most of us know that suppressing, denying, or ignoring anger doesn't work, either. If you bottle it up inside and try to forget about it, eventually it will burst forth, perhaps at—surprise!—your spouse or brother or co-worker. Or, instead of bursting forth, it may fester inside, creating depression or self-loathing or shame.

Is there another way to deal with anger? Yes. Instead of venting or suppressing it, investigate it. Simply notice the anger, accept its existence, and look at how it is affecting you. Examine where it comes from.

Eventually you will see that, beneath your anger, something is out of kilter. You are angry because you are not accurately perceiving the world. Instead, an unskillful belief is operating.

When another driver cuts you off in traffic, it's easy to imagine that they "made" you mad. But, really, you made yourself mad. Maybe you're angry because you believe you're entitled to a world in which no one ever violates the rules of the road. You already see how unrealistic this belief is.

This doesn't mean that you have to give up your belief in what is right. It's wise to believe that people ought to obey the rules of the road. But it is unrealistic to bank your happiness on everyone doing so. *The problem belief is the one that requires the world to always be the way you want in order for you to be happy.* Even if the way you want it to be is "right" or "fair" or "reasonable."

Every time the world "fails" us by not meeting our expectations, most of us choose to make ourselves mad. Yet *we already know* that the world won't always behave the way we want it to.

The problem is in our expectations. And those are within our power to change.

The next time reality doesn't fit with what you expect, and you see yourself starting to get mad, simply watch as that anger arises—without judging it, feeding it, or trying to push it away.

Then, instead of making yourself madder, examine the belief or expectation that is at the heart of your anger. You will always find that the belief can be changed to a more realistic or skillful one.

For example, if a driver cuts you off, perhaps they didn't mean to, and were briefly just careless. Or maybe the driver is rushing his pregnant wife to the hospital, and his concern for her welfare is paramount.

The next time you get cut off, immediately imagine the driver taking his wife to the hospital. What happens to your anger when your belief changes?

You will be happier if you change your beliefs to more realistic—or compassionate—ones. You will also put yourself in a mental state that enables you to make better decisions. All of this promotes your happiness—now and in the future.

15

Most of What We Fear is Imaginary

Do one thing every day that scares you.
—Eleanor Roosevelt

Fear is the result of a misguided imagination.
—Mark Twain

Fear is one of our greatest sources of unhappiness. It is the underlying cause of much of our anger, defensiveness, anxiety, and other unpleasant emotional states. Unfortunately, all too often it rules people's lives.

In and of itself, fear is not a problem. Fear is your instinctual reaction to a potentially dangerous situation. When that danger is real, fear can be helpful. You get scared when you see a car coming at you. Or, as happened to me recently, when a rattlesnake slithered in front of me across a hiking trail. Fear increases your blood pressure, so you have more oxygen to act quickly. It causes adrenaline to flow, so you quickly become very focused and alert. This hardwired reaction helps protect you from physical harm.

The source of much our fear, however, is not real. It comes from our own imaginations. We imagine what might happen, and then we fear what we imagine.

Yet, as we've already seen, most of what we imagine never comes to pass. When what we fear is imaginary, fear harms rather than helps us.

Our nervous system is biased a bit toward being fearful, because it is an instinct born of our cave-person heritage. There were dangerous things all around us then, so our bodies and minds are wired to be cautious.

But in modern times, we don't often encounter those kinds of actual dangers, like sabre tooth tigers or rattlesnakes. Today, most of our fears come from imagined dangers that will never come to pass.

So, fear does not often help. In fact, our habit of imagining frightening events creates anxiety, which is one of our biggest problems.

We open our credit card bill and see that it's much larger than we'd expected. Fear appears—and our proliferating thoughts take over: *How am I going to pay this? I won't be able to pay my other bills. What if I don't get the overtime I was promised this month? I'll lose the house!*

What's wrong with this picture? Our imagination caused us to react to the bill as if we'd seen a rattlesnake. Then it created a fantasy chain of events, which produced still more fear.

If you encounter an actual rattlesnake, your fear will help you get out of danger. You'll back away; or you'll try to fend it off or kill it; or you'll freeze and let it slither past you. Fear immediately activates your fight, flight, or freeze response. Then, when the danger has passed, your fear will naturally subside. Your system returns to normal.

But when fear is purely a response to a thought about the future—the exam you will soon take, the speech you need to give, or the difficult choice you have to make—you can't fight or flee from the danger, because it's entirely in your head. It's not even here yet. And it may *never* be here.

As a result, the fear doesn't go away. You're left with a pounding heart, elevated blood pressure, and ongoing anxiety.

That alone is painful enough. But often our proliferating thoughts produce all kinds of new and frightening fantasies. *What will Abigail say when she sees the size of this bill? We'll have a big fight. She'll storm off and stay with her mother. We'll get divorced. She'll try to get sole custody of the kids. They'll grow up damaged and miserable.* Your imagination has created a doomsday scenario—but all that's actually happened is you opened a credit card bill.

There are two important concerns here. First, the source of your fear was imaginary—entirely self-created. There was no rattlesnake, no physical danger.

Second, the mental stories you imagined made the fear worse, not better.

This internal fear-mongering habit can sap our energy and time, heighten our anxiety, and reduce our happiness and clarity of thought. It's like pouring sewage into a partly-filled pail of clear water: the sewage colors everything in the pail.

But this approach to fear isn't inevitable. You can choose to relate to fear in an entirely different way. You can make your fear support your happiness, rather than work against it. Here's how:

First, recognize that fear is not something to be avoided. You can't do away with it. Even if you could, that would not serve you well.

Fear is always sending you a message. You need to figure out, first, whether that message is based on reality, and, second, how to properly respond to that message.

The fear of a rattlesnake that you see or hear is based on reality. So is your fear of the car you see bearing down on you, or your fear of the man you see pointing a gun at you. In fact, in most cases when the dangerous event is real, you act instinctively and the fear subsides quickly when the danger passes. So the fear itself is no problem at all.

But the fear of something you imagine *might* be there, but have no evidence for, is a fantasy. When this kind of fear arises, identify it as such. Remind yourself that adrenaline and heightened anxiety won't help you when there's no actual here-and-now danger.

Then, instead of following your fantasy, follow your breath. Breathe slowly and deeply, and simply watch your breath as it enters and fills your lungs, then flows back out of your body.

As for the fear, simply watch that, too. Don't try to get rid of it, and don't be alarmed by it. And then investigate it—calmly look at its origins. In this way you can feel the fear, see that its source is imaginary, and watch it dissipate—usually sooner rather than later.

Let's examine a common fear, such as the fear of doing badly on the SATs or ACTs. Getting a low score isn't going to create any physical danger—but it might keep you from getting into the colleges you most want to attend. That potential loss may generate a small amount of fear. This is fine. Let yourself feel the fear, and use it as a motivating force to prepare thoroughly for the exam.

But if your imagination starts to create a fantasy scenario—*I'll do badly, end up at the local technical college, and spend forty years soldering circuit boards*—don't let yourself be drawn into it. Gently bring yourself back to your breath, to your body, and to the here and now. If necessary, do this multiple times, until you are anchored in the present.

When you think about doing something that seems difficult or challenging, fear will often arise. At first you may have the impulse to reduce this fear by avoiding the challenge or difficulty. But this is rarely the wisest path. For one thing, the difficulty or challenge may be unavoidable. Or it may be the very best thing for you to do. The only reason it's frightening is that it's new, and therefore unfamiliar.

Instead of trying to avoid it, simply stay present and watch the fear as it arises. Don't try to run from it or push it away. Let yourself feel it fully, without trying to do anything about it.

Then, calmly, ask yourself, *What is the source of this fear? Is it reality? Or is it my imagination?*

If it's reality, pay attention to the fear and do what it tells you.

But if it's your imagination, then bring yourself back to your body, to the present, and to your actual situation.

As you'll discover, many times the best thing to do is go right into the fear. Sometimes the fear is a signal to you to push your boundaries, and try something new or different, even if you think it is hard. Some difficulties or challenges will turn out not to be so hard after all.

Other situations and decisions *will* be challenging or difficult. But they will also teach you a great deal—and you will be wiser, stronger, more loving, or more capable because you have faced your fear and accepted the challenge.

So do not be afraid of fear—it is a very useful instinct if we relate to it skillfully.

16

Caring, Planning, and Worrying Are Three Different Things

---

*Most of the worst things I experienced in my life
never happened.*
—Mark Twain

---

*Worry does not empty tomorrow of its sorrow,
it empties today of its strength.*
—Corrie ten Boom

What is there to worry about? Nothing.

Caring, concern, planning, and strategizing can all help us deal with the future. A small amount of realistic fear can help, too, by keeping us focused.

But worry—obsessing over things that we have no ability to control—does no one any good.

As we've already seen, 90% of what we worry about never comes to pass—or, if it does, it turns out not to be as troublesome as we feared. Sometimes, in fact, it turns out to be beneficial.

One helpful way to look at worry is as an unmindful response to fear. When fear shows up, we climb aboard it, ride it into our imagination, and then jump-start the proliferation of thoughts. Soon worry crowds out everything else from our mind.

Anxiety is a lower-level kind of worry, but it is worry nonetheless. It allows our fear to control our attention, and feeds thoughts which are untrue, and not in our best interest to promote.

Worry and anxiety can eat up huge amounts of time and energy. They distract us from other things, many of which would bring us happiness and satisfaction. They hinder us in planning for the future. And they tend to generate more worry.

Our culture teaches us that worry is a natural part of caring. We're told that if we care about someone, we need to worry about them. If we don't worry about them, this means we don't care—or care enough.

This is nonsense. In fact, worry only gets in the way of caring.

If you care about someone, then one of the ways you can express that care is by not wasting your time and energy worrying about them. Instead, use that time and energy to engage with them and help them.

By all means plan, think things through, consider your options, and examine multiple scenarios for the future. Care deeply about the world and the people in it. And then act on those plans and your caring intentions.

But please let go of the worry habit. Worry will inhibit your ability to act, and make you unhappy in the meantime.

17

Feeling Bored is Boring; Instead, Have a Sense of Wonder and Awe

There is no scarcity of things to appreciate, just a scarcity of moments [in which] we are capable of such appreciation.
—Jack Kornfield

Live the mystery by beginning to perceive what average eyes fail to notice.
—Dan Millman

We live in an age of incredible access to things to do. When we feel bored, it's not because we don't have options. It's because our mind is focused too narrowly.

There are two aspects to this. The first is the belief that we need something else, something new, something pleasing, in order to be happy.

We're already seen that this approach to life—and the chasing and grasping that it involves—creates unhappiness, not happiness.

Second, when we are bored, we are simply not seeing the world the way it really is.

No matter what situation we find ourselves in, that moment is full of wonder, awe, and amazement. We only need to notice. Boredom is a message to start noticing.

I live near Torrey Pines, a large nature preserve just outside of San Diego. Torrey Pines has a huge lagoon, miles of hiking trails, bluffs that overlook the Pacific Ocean, and some of the greatest natural beauty in the world.

Yet many people who live nearby never go there. Some of them tell me that they can't, because they're too busy with other things, such as surfing the internet, playing video games, or answering texts and e-mails.

When some of these folks finally turn off their computers, they tell me that they're bored.

Where does this boredom come from? The world, with its immense beauty and wonder? Or their own minds?

Next time you're bored, don't look for something to relieve the boredom. Instead, look to what's already around you. Or in you. Don't look *at* it; look *into* it, with openness and curiosity. Don't judge it, or explain it, or try to get anything from it; just experience it.

That experience will be anything but boring.

In each moment, you have a choice:

You can open yourself to the world, and its majesty and mystery, not knowing what you'll discover, and not hoping for any particular outcome. Or...

You can identify those few specific things that you believe will relieve your boredom, and then work hard to acquire them. Of course, if you fail to acquire them, you'll make yourself bored and disappointed. And if you do acquire them but they don't live up to your expectations time after time, you'll also make yourself bored and disappointed.

Which choice sounds more potentially fulfilling?

18

Complaining and Blaming Are Not Skillful— Taking a Stand Is

Complainers change their complaints, but they never reduce the amount of time spent in complaining.
—Mason Cooley

You take your life in your own hands, and what happens? A terrible thing, no one to blame.
—Erica Jong

There's someone who works out at my gym who epitomizes Mason Cooley's quote. I often find her on the treadmill next to me.

Two years ago, this was her regular complaint: "My husband isn't very busy at work, so we have less money. I don't get my nails done as often, and we only took a vacation to the desert this year. I know the recession is largely the cause, but his boss doesn't appreciate him."

This year she has a new complaint that she repeats: "Fred is so busy at work. He barely has time to do things with us. When we went to Barbados on vacation, we could only go for a week because he had to get right back. His boss really doesn't appreciate how hard he works."

How happy would you say this woman is?

To be clear (and to be fair), there's an entirely different—and often helpful and purposeful—activity that's also called complaining. This involves acting in the service of positive change—for example, writing your Congressperson to support a proposed bill, or sitting down with your boss to suggest a way to create better results. This form of complaining can be quite valuable.

So when I say that complaining isn't skillful, I'm speaking of what the woman at my gym does: 1) whine about the current situation 2) to people who have no power to influence it 3) without creating a plan, intent, or willingness to change it.

Blaming is a close cousin of this type of complaining. By blaming, I don't mean respectfully calling out people who fail to fulfill their responsibilities. That can be both positive and skillful. I'm talking about assigning sole responsibility for your happiness to some entity other than yourself.

Blaming usually boils down to this accusation: *You did something that "made" me unhappy.* Paired with this accusation is the belief that you will not and cannot be happy until the situation changes—and that it is the other person's responsibility to change it for you.

Blaming and complaining are immense obstacles to happiness—both your own and that of the people around you. Both can keep you stuck in painful situations, because you abdicate the responsibility for change to someone else. Together, they're an almost-perfect recipe for dissatisfaction. You could call it a form of insanity.

Suppose you're unhappy about the way your boss treats you. She makes unreasonable demands, and often expresses them in rude, unprofessional ways. You have several options:

You can blame her for your unhappiness. This means you won't be happy until and unless she changes. It also means that if she doesn't change, you've condemned yourself to continued unhappiness.

You can complain to others about her. This does nothing to change your relationship with her. It also does nothing to change how you relate to the situation. Once again you've condemned yourself to unhappiness. You've also spread some of that unhappiness to others.

You can blame her and complain to others. But when you put blaming and complaining together, you may create a downward spiral. Nothing about the painful situation will change—except your dissatisfaction, which will probably get worse.

Fortunately, you have other options, all of which involve taking positive action—and taking a stand. You can speak to your boss honestly and directly about your concerns. Or you can invite her and her family to dinner, to create a more cordial and personal connection. Or you can set clear, firm boundaries with her, including specific consequences for crossing them (with the understanding that this might get you punished or fired).

All of these options involve looking at the situation as a challenge rather than a punishment—and all involve you acting to change the unhelpful dynamic.

What if it becomes clear that your boss or your situation won't or can't change, no matter what you do? First, you can accept that this is so. But even then, you get to decide what to do. You can send an e-mail to your boss's superior about her actions. You can try to get transferred to a different job or department or location. You can look for a new job. You can look into retiring sooner, or working part time. You can let go of trying to get satisfaction from your job, and look for it elsewhere—in volunteer work, or a hobby, or a spiritual or community group. You can start a file that documents your boss's mistreatment, and consult with an employment lawyer. Or you can simply decide to let things continue as they are, at least for now.

You can always choose skillful action over mere complaining or blaming.

If you don't like the policies of your state's governor, do what you can to change them—either the policies or the governor. If your partner watches TV all weekend instead of doing things with you, talk to them about how you feel and what you want—or accept that this is their preference and make your own weekend plans.

You've seen the bumper stickers on dog-owners' cars that say *Bark Less; Wag More*. We need a similar bumper sticker for humans: *Whine Less; Act Wisely*.

19

Use Your Mistakes to Your Advantage

Mistakes are part of life; everyone makes them, everyone regrets them. But some learn from them and some end up making them again. It's up to you to decide if you'll use your mistakes to your advantage.
—Meredith Sapp

Guilt is feeling bad about something you did. Shame is feeling bad about who you are—or, more accurately, who you *think* you are.

We feel guilty when we don't live up to our own values and standards. We tell a comforting lie instead of the difficult truth. We agree to do something but don't follow through. We say nothing when a co-worker makes a racist remark. We overeat when we promised ourselves we would not.

If you consistently fail to live according to your own values, you may eventually stop feeling that your *actions* have fallen short.

Instead, you may feel that *you* are inherently worthless or broken. At this point, your guilt has morphed into shame.

Both shame and guilt focus on our failures, and both cause us to review our past conduct, perhaps repeatedly. As a result, both cause suffering in the present.

Shame is particularly pernicious, because it inhibits our ability to change. After all, if we feel we are inherently worthless, then why change, since any effort to change will be futile?

Actually, the mistakes we've made can be very useful, if we choose to learn from them. But guilt and shame prevent us from using our mistakes to our advantage. They can help cause some of our mistakes to become patterns of behavior—addictions—and become even more difficult to change.

Fortunately, we have another, more positive option: remorse.

Remorse is a signal that you need to change something in order to be happier in life. It also looks at the past as a learning experience. First, you recognize and acknowledge what you did. Then you mindfully investigate the emotions, impulses, thoughts, and habits behind your actions. You acknowledge the harm your actions caused. You regret what you did. Depending on the circumstances, you may apologize to the person or people you harmed. You may also offer to make amends to them.

But, most important, *you use this awareness of what happened, and why, to change the way you think and act.*

Let's imagine that you've gained weight over the last few years. You use eating as a salve to heal emotional upsets in your life. It has become a mindless pattern as well—you sit in front of the TV set and eat without being at all mindful of what you are eating, or how much. This is very common in the United States.

You want to change, but you feel guilty about your weight gain, and maybe you're even ashamed about your appearance. The guilt and shame actually stand in your way, because they make you feel bad about yourself. This encourages you to return to the very behavior you are trying to change.

This same pattern can happen with alcohol, drugs, the internet, shopping, romantic partners, and plenty of other things. Guilt and shame obstruct change rather than promote it.

Remorse, however, encourages change. It allows you to see that your behavior is not you—it is just a pattern you have acquired, like an old sweater that doesn't fit well or feel good anymore. Once you recognize a behavior pattern for what it is, you can begin the process of letting it go.

Unlike guilt and shame—which focus on you, your failures, and your past—remorse focuses on healing, positive change, and the future.

The next time you do something you regret, or realize you are stuck in an unhelpful pattern of behavior, bypass the guilt and shame. Instead, embrace remorse. It is one of the first and best steps to a better life.

20

Doing Nothing is Highly Underrated

Mindfulness is the agent of our freedom. Through mindfulness we arrive at faith, we grow in wisdom, and we attain equanimity.
—Sharon Salzberg

So how do we stop worry? How do we not wallow in anger? How do we not get stuck in hopelessness or depression? How do we use fear to our advantage, rather than letting it rule us? How do we choose remorse over guilt or shame?

By doing nothing.

Doing nothing is extremely underrated. In fact, it is often the best way out of unhappy mental places.

As we've seen, we find our way into painful mind states—depression, anxiety, anger, guilt—through our reactions, which are usually based on false core beliefs. Over time, those reactions can become habits—conditioned patterns. We do the same painful thing over and over.

What if, instead, we did nothing? This means *not* reacting according to our usual pattern, and, instead, simply allowing things to happen. Even when—*especially when*—what happens is not what we want.

When things don't go as we'd like, much of the time we immediately form a judgment about our situation, label it, and react to it in the same way we reacted to similarly labeled situations in the past. When we do this, we stop being open to the many aspects and opportunities before us. Instead, we turn our attention to how "bad" or "horrible" the situation is, and to how we might change or escape it. We do this time and time again.

By doing nothing, you can break that pattern.

When I say "doing nothing," I don't mean ignoring the situation— or the emotions that arise. *I mean the opposite.* I mean giving your full attention and awareness to the situation.

This includes closely inspecting your immediate feelings, *without judgment, labeling, or reaction.* Instead of venting or avoiding or calculating, you simply observe and investigate. You apply your attention and awareness to the event as it unfolds around you, as well as to what unfolds inside you. You notice your judgments and impulses as they arise, but don't act on them.

Imagine that you're driving in heavy traffic. It's moving much slower than you want, and no alternate route is available. You can tell yourself that you're in a "bad" situation. You can worry that you will be late to an important meeting. You can blame someone— transportation planners, other drivers, the construction crew up ahead—for the traffic. You can try to rush—although you can go no faster than the cars in front of you. You can imagine how people will be mad at you for being late, and how this will ruin your chances of a promotion. Soon you find yourself lost in anxiety and worry.

And none of the thoughts listed above would get you out of that anxiety. Indeed, thinking only propelled you further into it.

But what if, instead, you were to do nothing? What if you were to accept the situation with full attention and awareness—but *without* reaction or judgment, or projections from the past, or fantasies about the future? What if you were simply present with the situation, and with your feelings about it? What if you were to approach those feelings with curiosity and a willingness to investigate them, rather than with an imagined need to fix them or get rid of them?

For starters, you'll see your situation more clearly. You'll realize that nothing you can do, think, feel, or imagine will make the traffic get better. And maybe, as a result, you can relax.

By doing nothing except noticing what's happening—including what you're feeling and thinking—you can see how much of your anxiety didn't actually come from the situation, but from your own projection and fantasies about it.

We looked at this process of mental proliferation in earlier chapters. Ninety-nine percent of our anxiety comes from this proliferation.

Doing nothing stops proliferation in its tracks.

Other things become possible when you do nothing. You can learn from the situation. (*In the future, I'll take the train until the construction is finished.*) You can learn about yourself. (*When I feel frustrated, it's not necessarily a problem I need to solve. I can just let myself feel frustrated for a while, and after a few minutes that feeling will usually go away on its own.*) You can learn about your beliefs and preconceived notions. (*I'm pretty quick to blame the government for almost everything I don't like. God knows the government has problems, but it isn't the evil, all-destroying empire I created in my imagination.)* You can gain perspective on the situation and realize that it is nowhere near as bad as you are making it. (*My situation isn't so bad. I'm sitting in a comfortable seat, in an air-conditioned car, with a book on tape and a radio.)*

Doing nothing is not always easy. In fact, at first it's difficult. Like anything else, it takes practice. But over time it will get easier, and you'll get better at it. It's like learning to ride a bike, or play an instrument, or cook a soufflé.

Doing nothing is always an available option.

So, how do you practice doing nothing?

You can do it almost any time or anywhere, though a quiet, peaceful spot is best. You can be in almost any body position, but I (and many other people who practice doing nothing) recommend sitting on a cushion, a chair, or a sofa, with your back straight.

For 20 minutes a day, sit quietly in this position. Simply breathe and pay attention to your breath.

As thoughts jump into your head, just watch them. Bring your awareness and attention to them, then let them go without dwelling on them, or engaging with them, or reacting to them.

By the way, another name for doing nothing—paying full attention to what is happening, without judgment or reactivity—is mindfulness.

21

Fortunately, Life Has a Reset Button

People usually consider walking on water or in thin air a miracle. But I think the real miracle is not to walk either on water or in thin air, but to walk on earth. Every day we are engaged in a miracle which we don't even recognize: a blue sky, white clouds, green leaves, the black, curious eyes of a child—our own two eyes. All is a miracle.

—Thich Nhat Hanh

Computers, game consoles, and most other electronic gadgets have reset buttons. If the device gets hung up, you simply push the button, reboot it, and—voila!—you're back in business.

Life has one of those buttons as well—in fact, several of them— but most of us don't realize it. You can use one of them whenever you get stuck in a painful place. They are particularly useful when you're feeling hopeless or inadequate.

If you use one or more of the buttons often enough, you can experience the perspective that Thich Nhat Hanh has on life.

Painful feelings can arise when you're in a difficult situation that seems—and, in fact, may be—impossible to change. You lose your job when your company downsizes. You have a serious health problem. Your boyfriend or girlfriend dumps you for someone else. A close friend or family member dies.

That's how the hopelessness often begins. And once we feel that our situation is hopeless, we can spiral down into ever more hopelessness.

Some people try to counteract hopelessness through alcohol, drugs, or addictive behavior (shopping, gambling, porn, etc.). These are all attempts to reboot our life through some strong, pleasant, short-term stimulation. Often they work—for the short term. But they never work over the long term, and they come with some very negative side effects. Although they very briefly provide some good feelings, and they may temporarily numb or blunt the suffering, they mostly feed the downward spiral into greater hopelessness.

Fortunately, you have another option—one that can lift you out of hopelessness and into hope. It has two aspects. One I've already discussed: mindfulness or awareness. The other is perspective.

Up until now, I've talked about using awareness to help you stay present and get out of your mental stories. But you can also use your awareness to shift *what you focus on*—to change your perspective.

Like mindfulness itself, changing your perspective is a skill that can be learned, practiced, and deepened.

An excellent introduction to the power and practice of shifting perspective is Andy Andrews' novel *The Noticer*. The protagonist of this novel is a mysterious old gentleman who shows up in the lives of strangers who feel stuck in seemingly hopeless situations. He helps people get unstuck by encouraging them to be aware—to notice things they hadn't noticed before.

For example, one character in the novel is an aging woman whose husband has died. She is deeply depressed, and feels that life is not worth living anymore. The protagonist helps this woman notice some of the positive things already in her life: her children, who still love her; her good health; and the natural beauty surrounding her home. All of these things were already present—but, because of her perspective and beliefs, she simply didn't see them.

Many of us have the same problem as the characters in *The Noticer*: we focus on a single limited aspect of life, and get stuck there. We see this in the person who devotes their life to finding the perfect partner; the person who is obsessed with their home, or job, or business, or kids, or hobby; the fitness fanatic who spends most of the day at the gym; and the religious zealot who spends every waking moment following each nuance prescribed by their sect.

We also see this with folks who get caught in hopelessness. Their own hopelessness eventually becomes the biggest—or the only—thing they notice. Eventually it becomes their life.

But a limited perspective isn't permanent or unchangeable. Even if you're caught in hopelessness, you can still recognize your situation and reset your perspective.

Later chapters will look at several different reset buttons, all of which help us realize that whatever we're stuck in is not the whole of our life.

One wonderful reset button is gratitude. Start the day by spending just 10 minutes listing all the things you're grateful for. Each day, actually write down your list—and, for each item on it, write a short sentence about *why* you are grateful.

You can of course repeat items from earlier lists—but when you honestly reflect, you'll discover hundreds of things to be grateful for in your life.

There will be periods in your life when you'll need to use this and other reset buttons often—maybe even multiple times on the same day. That's okay. No one's counting, and there's no limit on your use of the buttons. In fact, as you'll discover, the more you use them, the more of life's daily miracles will be revealed to you.

22

Actions Matter—a Lot— But They Always Start With Intention

At first there is an intention
The intention turns into the thought
The thought turns into the word
The word turns into the deed
The deed turns into one's habit
The habit turns into one's character
Your character shapes your destiny
—Lao Tzu

Although doing nothing is underrated, please don't get the impression that doing something is unimportant. Everything we do matters. In fact, every single thing we do starts a chain reaction that creates far-reaching ripples in the waters of life.

This awareness leads to two general principles about the world—principles we often ignore. And you already know what happens when we ignore reality: we bump (or sometimes crash) into it, and we get hurt.

The first principle is that, while everything we do matters a great deal, our actions alone do not dictate the results we want. The rest of the universe has a lot to say about how things turn out. The outcomes of our actions are never fully within our control.

Second, our actions spring from our intentions—but we're not always aware of those intentions. Much of what we do is done mindlessly, thoughtlessly, as a result of an ingrained or automatic habit. There is still an underlying intention, but we are not aware of it.

Our actions can make us aware of our intentions, if we pay attention to them. This creates the possibility for changing our intentions. This can have far-reaching implications.

When you carefully examine your actions, and the thoughts that prompt them, you can discern the underlying intention that is operating. You can then evaluate that intention to see whether it contributes to your long-term happiness. In some cases, you may also discover that you've been operating according to an intention you don't actually want to have.

Imagine that you're hungry, so you grab a pickle from the pickle jar in the fridge. But you're in a hurry, so you don't put the lid on carefully. Your intention—which you may not be aware of right then—is to hurry, because you want to get someplace other than where you are at the moment. So you put the lid on quickly, but not correctly.

Two weeks later, as you prepare dinner, you take out the pickle jar, grabbing it by the top. But the top is loose—the result of your action two weeks before—and the jar drops on the floor and shatters.

Meanwhile, your kids are shouting, "I'm hungry! Where's dinner?" So, hurriedly—and again not very carefully or mindfully—you sweep up the glass and finish cooking.

The next morning, when you wake up, you walk barefoot into the kitchen. You step on a big piece of broken glass, which cuts deeply into your foot. Fifteen minutes later you're in the emergency room.

All of this suffering sprang from one simple intention—the intention to hurry rather than be attentive and present in the moment. At the time, you weren't even aware of this intention to hurry. Yet it partly shaped your destiny.

Everything matters. Acting mindfully and skillfully in the present tends to yield positive results in the future. Acting unmindfully or unskillfully tends to create not-so-positive results.

Wisdom is the ability to choose *right now* the intentions, thoughts, and actions which will promote future happiness.

This is actually the notion of karma. Choosing a skillful intention or goal, and then skillful actions furthering it, will promote, but not guarantee, a skillful result. It's like planting seeds—if you plant apple seeds, water them, and care for them, there is a good chance you will get an apple tree. It is not guaranteed—the weather and other conditions out of your control have a lot to do with it. But if you select a different kind of seeds, or fail to care properly and mindfully for the apple seeds, you will not get the apple tree.

If you'd been more mindful of your intention with the pickle jar—*Wait a minute, I'm rushing around here without paying attention*—then you might have caught yourself and changed your intention. *You know what? Paying attention to what I'm doing is more important than moving fast.* And things probably would have turned out differently. *Wait a second—something feels funny about this pickle jar. I'd better undo the lid and screw it back on again.*

One great thing about karma is we can always change it. While it is true that our past intentions and actions affect our present, it is also true that we can at any moment change them. Regardless of what has happened, next time we can be mindful of our intentions, and actions, with the pickle jar—and all other things in our life as well.

When you don't pay attention, you may simply react. You yell at your spouse when they do something you don't like. You feel depressed, so you go shopping, or drinking. A driver cuts you off, so you get angry.

But through a simple act of mindfulness, you can discern your underlying intention and change it. That, in turn, can change your actions—and what happens thereafter. Thus this simple act of awareness can change your life—and the lives of those around you—for the better.

23

You Have a Quarter of a Second to Choose Your Intention

In the West, there's a myth that freedom means free expression—that to follow all desires wherever they take one is true freedom. In fact, as one observes the mind, one sees that following desires, attractions, repulsions is not at all freedom, but is a kind of bondage. A mind filled with desires and grasping inevitably entails great suffering. Freedom is not to be gained through the ability to perform certain external actions. True freedom is an inward state of being. Once it is attained, no situation in the world can bind one or limit one's freedom.

—Jack Kornfield

H appiness has a lot to do with freedom—freedom in the sense that Kornfield talks about on the previous page. And we are not free when we aren't acting in accord with our deepest intentions or values.

If we practice mindfulness and use our wisdom, the intentions we follow will be largely determined by our values. But if we are not mindful, they will be largely determined by habit.

When we act purely out of habit, we often act from a shallow intention—an intention to hurry, to make things easy, or to avoid short-term discomfort. These are not wise intentions. As a result, we only frustrate ourselves in the long run.

Because we're human, we often have competing intentions. We intend to be careful about what we eat, to be nice to our sister, to exercise, and to read two chapters of that book on our homework list. But we also have a desire to eat that bag of Oreos, snap at our sister when she's late for the umpteenth time, take a long nap, and spend time online instead of reading. Over time, most of us also develop habits that encourage us to follow these shallower desires.

Our culture actively promotes these shallow desires. Just look at *People* magazine or the ads on TV. But we all have deeper desires as well—desires that promote long-term happiness. We want to be kind. We want to do well at work or in school. We want to help others succeed. We want to get our body in good condition. We know that if we act in accord with these intentions, they will support our long-term happiness.

But sometimes we reach the end of the day without acting from any of these deeper intentions. Instead, we spent a lot of time online, ate a big bag of chips, went shopping, and watched TV.

Now we don't feel so good. Our first response—and, perhaps, our habit—is to try to ignore that dissatisfaction.

But what if, instead, we were to calmly and mindfully look at that dissatisfaction—that anxiety, or unease, or depression?

As we look closely, without judgment, we see that our dissatisfaction comes from not acting in accord with our deeper intentions. We have allowed our shallower intentions—or our habits, or the norms of our culture, or the people we hang with—to distract us.

We are not free when we act according to these myriad influences. We are letting our life be controlled by mindless habits, rather than by those intentions that are aligned with our deepest values.

The great news is that we can choose which intentions to follow, and align them with our true values. This means that we can access freedom—and plant the seeds for future happiness—simply by making a mindful choice.

It turns out that we have a quarter-of-a-second window of freedom. This does not sound like much, but if we are mindful, we can expand that window a great deal.

Neurologists have studied how people are moved to act. The chain of events goes like this:

First there is a stimulus. This can be external (a car driving toward you; someone shouting at you; the smell of popcorn) or internal (the memory of a friend's smile; a pang of hunger; a pang of regret).

Second, there is our immediate internal response to that stimulus—often a desire or an aversion. We may like it (*that suit is a beautiful blue*), or dislike it (*that's an ugly blue*), or be neutral about it (*it's blue*). If we like it, we typically want to hang onto the experience. If we don't, we usually want to push it away. If it's neutral, we may be bored or uninterested in it.

Third, a thought—or one of our internal stories—might arise. *I'll never have a sense of style or fashion*. Or, *I don't look good in suits*. This can start the proliferation of thoughts.

Fourth, we decide how to act. We might do something in response to the initial stimulus (we keep looking at the woman in the suit), or to our desire or aversion (we smile and shout, "Nice suit!"), or to our internal story (we look down and think, *I've got the totally wrong body type to wear suits*).

There's another possibility. If we feel aversion, or if our internal story is painful, we may do none of these. Instead, we may try to withdraw or escape or distract ourselves—perhaps by looking away, or mentally dissing the person in the suit (*There goes another rich bitch*), or deciding to get a sandwich or a glass of wine.

This all happens in a quarter of one second. But in that brief window of time, if we are mindful of this whole process, we can choose our intention—and our wisest action.

Better still, we can learn to expand that window of time. This gives us a chance to consider what action fits with our deepest values, and what is in our—and others'—long-term best interests.

When we do this repeatedly, our life is no longer a series of automatic actions dictated by habits and patterns, or desires and aversion, or inaccurate beliefs and internal stories about the world. Instead, we make mindful decisions and act in ways that reflect our deeper values and intentions.

One way to expand your quarter-second window is to practice observing this entire sequence carefully—from stimulus to thought to intention to action—without judgment, until you have a bird's-eye view of the whole process.

This observation puts the whole process into slow motion—in effect, expanding your window of time for changing your intention and choosing your action (or lack of action) wisely.

This is not some mystical practice, like a trance. It's the opposite. It's a way to help you become aware of what is actually going on—

and, thus, to choose your intentions, your actions, and the outcomes you would like to encourage.

As you practice this over time, you'll also realize that observation alone is often enough. You don't have to act on every thought that shows up. You can choose to do nothing. You can simply watch without judging or reacting.

Or you can, when you are ready, choose to exercise a wise choice. The next few chapters talk about how to discern what is wise.

Your life is a series of these quarter seconds—these present moments. You can use these moments to be mindful and to make wise choices. Or not.

24

Anchor Your Life to What You Value

---

*Happiness is that state of consciousness which proceeds from
the achievement of one's values.*

—Ayn Rand

I f you line up your intentions and actions with wisely selected values,
you will promote your own happiness. If you act in a way that's
inconsistent with wisely selected values, you won't. It's that simple.

So plan your days—and your life—around what you value most.
Then set your intention to live according to those values, because
your intentions partly determine how you will meet each moment.

What should your deepest values be? I can't pick them for you—
nor should I. But many great thinkers have articulated them in various
ways. The list below is a very brief, helpful, and widely accepted
(but certainly not exhaustive) one. Each value can be expressed as a
prohibition or an encouragement—a negative or positive articulation
of the value:

1. Don't harm others—or yourself. Not doing harm includes not intentionally killing any living being. The positive way of expressing this value is to respect the value of all living beings, and be kind and considerate to them.

If each action we take has behind it an intention not to do harm, think how different our life—and our world—would be.

If this is the only value you live by, it's enough. All the other principles below follow from the basic value of kindness.

2. Don't take anything that is not offered to you. The most basic form of this principle is not to steal. The positive manifestation is generosity, having a spirit of giving.

3. Don't cause harm through sexual misconduct. This principle doesn't disapprove of sex; it simply cautions against sexual activity that harms people (including yourself). Another way of thinking about it is showing respect for all human beings, and for yourself.

4. Don't cause harm through the use of intoxicants. I've personally experienced the consequences of not following this principle. I can tell you from painful experience that they can be severe.

The positive principle includes a commitment to awareness. It's impossible to be fully aware of our intentions and values when we misuse intoxicants. We can't possibly see what is really going on when we distort our consciousness with them.

5. Don't lie. Speak the truth. Be honest in all your dealings with the world—and with yourself.

The above list was created by a man named Siddhartha Gotama, who lived about 2500 years ago. He came to be known as the Buddha, which means *one who is awake*, or *one who is aware*.

You can look at this list as a set of guidelines for human happiness. If you follow them, you're more likely to have a happy life—a life that's free from suffering. If you don't follow them, you're not likely to be happy over the long term.

One thing that I would add to this list, which was naturally part of people's lives 2500 years ago, but unfortunately is not today, is paying proper attention to your body through exercise and good nutrition. When the Buddha wrote these guidelines, there were no computers, cars, elevators, or fast food. People did not spend most of their waking hours sitting, as they do today. Instead, people walked everywhere. Indeed, the Buddha walked 10 or more miles a day, even in his advanced years. Taking care of one's body was a natural part of life.

It's a different world today. People get little exercise, and mostly eat processed foods, and too much of them. Most of us need to be mindful and deliberate about taking care of our bodies. But, like the other values on Gotama's list, this one flows from the principle of doing no harm—and following it naturally promotes our long-term happiness.

Anchor your life to what you value. Act according to your deepest intentions and values. And don't worry about what all this will get you, or whether you will achieve your agenda.

We cannot control everything—or, really, much of anything—in the world. The Universe has a lot to say about whether we fulfill our agenda.

But an amazing thing often happens when we align our actions with our wisely selected values and intentions. Often—not all the time, and not always quickly, but over the long haul—the world lines up with what we value and what we intend.

25

Determination and Discipline Lead to Freedom

A tree that fills a man's embrace grows from a seedling. A tower nine stories high starts with one brick. A journey of a thousand miles begins with a single step.
—Lao Tzu

Nothing in the world can take the place of persistence. Talent will not—nothing is more common than talented failures. Genius will not—unrewarded genius is almost a proverb. Education will not—the world is full of educated derelicts. Persistence and determination are omnipotent.
—Calvin Coolidge

t's not always easy to follow through on our intentions. We let our thoughts and emotions get in the way of action. We get caught up in excuses, blaming, fantasies, and false internal stories. And then there are those habits—and, sometimes, those addictions—that are so hard to change.

But simply taking that first step that Lao Tzu speaks of can break through it all. Taking that first step multiple times can change your life.

We've already seen how changing the way you relate to your thoughts can change what you think and do. It turns out that the opposite is also true: changing what you do can change what you think, replacing painful mental stories with empowerment.

There is actually a formula of sorts for this. One version of it appears in the book *The Monk Who Sold His Ferrari*. This is a modern-day fable about a successful trial lawyer who worked himself sick to the point of a heart attack. He worked far too much, disregarded what was really important in life, and put himself in a very unhealthy state. He then went to visit monks in India, studied with them, and came back to the U.S. with a completely different set of values and attitude.

He was able not only to change the way he thought about things, but he was also able to effect a fundamental change in his actions—from those which were leading him to ruin, to ones that promoted his long-term happiness. He was able to align his actions with his values and intentions—all in spite of his previous habits, and the social and cultural influences that pointed in the opposite direction.

The Monk Who Sold His Ferrari explains how determination and discipline lead to freedom—freedom from our false internal stories, our unhelpful habits, our painful conditioning, and our unrealistic thinking. It also offers a real-life example of how we can select actions that are free of harmful influences, and consistent with our deepest values and intentions.

But how do we get from having the thought, *I wish I would be more_____*, or *I wish I could get myself to be more _____*, to actually living a life embodying those values and intentions? You could fill in those blanks with anything you value—*loving, caring, fit, patient, generous.* How do we act in accord with that wish in the face of all our habits, prior mental patterns, and cultural norms and messages, all of which can get in our way?

The answer is determination and discipline.

There is an ancient word from the Pali language—*addhitana*—which really captures what I mean by determination. Literally translated, it means taking a special stand. It is often translated as determination—that is, a quality that makes you continue trying to achieve something that is difficult. Or it is also translated as resolve, which means to make a definite and serious decision to do something—or to find a solution to something. So what I am talking about in this chapter is all of these things—to find an answer or solution to something—to be free from those habits, addictions, and patterns that keep us from achieving our true highest intentions. And then to make a serious decision to act to make that solution happen, even in the face of difficulties—sometimes great difficulties. For short I will call this determination.

I'm not talking here about getting the house or car or partner or job you want, or think you want. (Although this formula can help us to achieve those kinds of goals as well.) But we already know that we cannot make the world line up with our desires all the time, or even much of the time. We also know that fulfilling our desires for external things doesn't dictate our happiness.

I am talking about applying this kind of determination to acting on your deepest intentions. This enables you to do what you say you will do, when you said you would do it. It helps you keep your commitments—to others, to yourself, and to your values. It empowers you to act in accord with those values and the intentions that flow from them.

So how do you build this kind of determination?

You do it by acting according to your values, regardless of the thoughts, stories, or fantasies that pop into your head to dissuade you. Over and over, you choose positive action over mental stories.

Making this choice is sometimes called discipline. You follow your chosen path even when stories try to point you in a different direction. When excuses tell you not to. When your friends or colleagues act otherwise, and try to get you to follow the crowd. When following your values will be difficult, but following the herd seems easier.

You'll recall from earlier chapters—and from your own brief experiment in Chapter 5—that you can't control your thoughts. But you *can* choose which thoughts to give your attention to, nurture, and encourage, and which ones to let go of.

Discipline strengthens and supports that choice.

Suppose you decide that you are going to get in better physical shape. You promise yourself that you will work out at the gym twice a week. The only time you have available is early in the morning, before work, so you plan to get up at 5:00 a.m. on Mondays and Thursdays.

On Monday morning, your alarm goes off. You wake up and look out the window. A stream of mental stories starts playing: *I'm too tired today. I went to bed late last night. Besides, it's foggy out, so I'll have to drive really slowly. Plus, my foot hurts.* If you keep your attention on these stories, they'll probably take over, and you'll be much less likely to get to the gym that day. That stream of thoughts may get the better of you.

But you have an alternative.

As the thoughts arise, don't hang onto them, or argue with them, or give them any energy. Don't believe them—they aren't true just because you think them. Let go of them as soon as they appear. For half a minute or so, let them arise and drift off like bubbles.

In short, start by doing nothing.

Then create a different stream of thoughts. Remember your commitment to take care of your body. Think about the increased energy you will have, and how much better your body will feel, if you get up and work out. Follow this thought stream for about half a minute.

Then get up. Act on your chosen intention.

And then do it again on Thursday. And then the following Monday. And so on.

Another way of thinking about determination and discipline is that they are *mindfulness turned into action.* Over time you develop a capacity for action based on long-term values rather than habits or short-term desires.

Discipline has gotten a bad rap. Most of us think of discipline in terms of being disciplined—i.e., punished—as children. In fact, when I looked up the word in a well-known dictionary, the first definition was *the practice of training people to obey rules or a code of behavior, using punishment to correct disobedience.*

But this is *not* the discipline I'm talking about. I'm referring to a later definition in that same dictionary: *training that corrects, molds, or perfects the mental faculties or moral character.* This is a path to freedom.

Discipline builds determination. Determination usually starts small, with nothing more than thoughts. But if you pay attention to the thoughts that support your deepest values and intentions, and let others drop by the wayside, you can effect positive changes in your life—and others' lives as well.

26

Failure Simply Means You Are Trying New Things

> *I didn't make any mistakes. I just know a thousand ways not to make a light bulb.*
> —Thomas Edison

> *You may be disappointed if you fail, but you are doomed if you don't try.*
> —Beverly Sills

Goals and dreams—and the passion to achieve them—are wonderful things. In fact, they are essential to our happiness.

But most people relate to them in an unrealistic way, often acting unwisely and making themselves miserable in the process.

On the one hand, goals and dreams provide us with focus, energy, and meaning. On the other, no matter how much passion you have, and no matter how hard you work, there's no guarantee that you'll achieve the results you desire.

But here's the part most people miss—and many find difficult to accept: *achieving your goals isn't essential to your happiness.*

Having goals is essential; achieving them is not.

Our culture teaches us to use goals as a carrot to spur us on, which is fine. But it also teaches us to use them as a stick to hit ourselves with when we don't succeed. If we set a goal and don't reach it, we're supposed to brand ourselves a failure and then blame ourselves (or others) for the "failure." We're supposed to use any and every unachieved goal to punish ourselves.

Is it any wonder why some people are afraid to set goals? Who wants to be an unhappy failure?

There is a wiser way to think about goals: as inspiration for ongoing improvement.

In Japan, this approach is embodied in the word *kaizen*. There is no corresponding word in English, but the phrase "constant, never-ending improvement" comes very close.

In each moment, you have the opportunity to be a little better than you were the day—and the moment—before. This is always your situation, whether you are four years old, or 14, or 44, or 104.

And if you don't reach a particular goal today, or tomorrow, or ever, you have still learned something from your effort and experience—and much of what you have learned will serve you well in the future.

Many great achievements were the result of people failing to reach their goals. Spencer Silver tried to invent an adhesive that had much greater strength than any previous glue. He failed miserably. But that adhesive became the key ingredient for a new, incredibly successful, invention: Post-It Notes. In 1853, chef George Crum grew frustrated when a diner sent back his fried potatoes multiple times, saying they were too thick and undercooked. So Crum cut a potato into paper-thin slices, fried the slices until they were brittle, and salted them—thus creating what became the country's most popular snack, the potato chip. Researcher Alexander Fleming searched long and hard for a wonder drug that could cure diseases, but success evaded him. Eventually Fleming threw away his experiments—but, as he did, he noticed that a contaminated Petri dish contained a mold that was dissolving the bacteria around it. He tried growing the mold by itself, and discovered the powerful antibiotic penicillin.

Other people achieved their goals only after repeated failures. Winston Churchill lost every election he ran in until he was elected prime minister of Britain at age 62. Oprah Winfrey was fired from her first television job, and was told that she was unfit for TV. After a year in the movies, Marilyn Monroe was dropped by her first producers because they thought she couldn't act. When Tori Amos sang her song "Leather" for a music industry mogul, he told her, "If you perform that song, you'll have no career." She performed it many times, and went on to become one of the most successful recording artists in history. Thomas Edison failed over a thousand times before creating one of the most life-changing inventions in history: the light bulb.

Many other people never achieved their goals at all—but their lives were deepened and strengthened by those goals, and by the steps they took to achieve them.

When you set a goal of your own and work toward it, you may reach it, or you may not. But either way you will be better off.

In case you're wondering, there's a difference between a goal and an intention. A goal is specific and measureable, and is set in the present but points toward the future. In contrast, an intention needn't be measureable, and it can often be achieved in the here and now. Building a successful carpentry business is a goal. So is bringing clean drinking water to remote Congolese villages. Both will likely take years to achieve. But meeting each moment with compassion, wisdom, and kindness is an intention, and it can be achieved right now—and then over and over again, moment after moment.

So, think of the relationship between goals and intentions as climbing a mountain. It's good to have a goal to climb to the top of a challenging peak. But you may or may not make it, and if you do there will be many other mountains that you may choose to climb.

But your intention as you take each step is extremely important. How you approach each step—how you meet each moment—matters more to your happiness than whether you achieve your goal.

27

Speaking is Like Pouring Concrete

Speech is the mirror of the soul; as a man speaks, so he is.
—Publilius Syrus

Your own words are the bricks and mortar of the dreams you want to realize. Your words are the greatest power you have. The words you choose and their use establish the life you experience.
—Sonia Choquette

ave you ever worked with concrete? I did a bit when I was a kid. When it is first poured, it is like oatmeal, easy to stir and shape. But as the hours pass, it gets firmer and firmer. After a day it has completely solidified, and the only way to reshape it is to break it up with a jackhammer or sledge. So the earlier you work with it, the easier it is to shape.

Our words and actions are like this, too. Speech is a type of action—indeed, it is the most common kind of action we take.

Speech always starts with an intention—but, as we have seen, we may not always be aware of our intention. So sometimes we say things that harm others, even though harming others is not one of our core values.

All of us have gotten upset with how someone acts toward us. But then we have a choice. We can react mindlessly by blurting unkind words toward them, thus venting our anger. Or we can consider what action (including holding our tongue) would most align with our values.

We have a similar choice when we don't feel good about ourselves. We can gossip or belittle or complain about others, in an effort to feel better about ourselves in comparison. Or we can ask ourselves what speech would most align with our values.

Most of us spend much of our time talking, e-mailing, and texting without being mindful of our intentions, or of the impact our words may have on others. This lack of mindfulness can create two problems.

First, belittling others, gossiping, or complaining can easily become habits. The more they harden, the more difficult it is to change them. In fact, over time, falling into this habit can be like pouring multiple of layers of concrete. Remember what Lao Tzu said: intention leads to thought, thought to word, word to deed, deed to character, and character to destiny.

Second, unmindful speech can hurt others. It can also create suffering for you when those people respond to your hurtful words.

The best time to be mindful of your speech is before your thoughts become words. The idea is to choose (or change) the path of the concrete before it hardens.

If you watch your thoughts carefully, they can reveal your intentions to you. If these are not the intentions you want to follow— that is, if they are not aligned your own essential values—you can catch yourself, change your intention, and change your words. This, in turn, could change your destiny.

Here are a few things to ask yourself as you watch your thoughts and discern your intention:

- Are the words you plan to say kind, or harsh and unkind?
- Are they truthful, or false or misleading?
- Are they useful in some way, or are they simply chatter?
- Are they likely to create harmony or connection among people, or are they likely to create separation or discord?

By choosing the words you speak to others wisely, you skillfully set your own direction through life.

28

What Should I Do for a Living?

> *If a man is called to be a street-sweeper, he should sweep streets even as Michelangelo painted or Beethoven composed music or Shakespeare wrote poetry. He should sweep streets so well that all the hosts of Heaven and Earth will pause and say, "Here lived a great street-sweeper who did his job well."*
> —Martin Luther King, Jr.

n America, most of us assume that we need to find and get the perfect job in order to be happy. And if the job turns out to be less than perfect, then we tell ourselves that we made the wrong choice.

This setup virtually guarantees us unhappiness.

As we saw at the beginning of this book, happiness isn't the result of what we acquire, whether it's a job, a partner, a house, a corner office, or a pony.

We also saw that the way we show up—the intention we bring to each moment—is often more important than what we do. This is exactly what Dr. King was speaking about in his description of a mindful street-sweeper. What you bring to your work often matters more than what it brings to you.

But there is another aspect of choosing a job or a career that you'll need to keep in mind: in doing your work, will you help others or harm others? Will you serve others in some way or will you simply take from them?

In practice, work that hurts others will eventually lead to your own unhappiness as well. Some of these jobs—arms smuggler, prostitute, drug dealer, pimp—are obvious. Others, such as jobs in sales or advertising that require you to deceive people, may not be so obviously or immediately pernicious.

The way in which you do your work also matters. For example, if you come to work each day knowing that you will be serving others, and that your job is a way to offer wisdom or compassion to others, you are much more likely to be happy—and to do your job well.

One other thing about jobs and career: don't stress out about making the right decision. Unlike many other things in life—such as your parents, your skin color, or your age—if you feel you have the wrong job, you can get a different one. Or, sometimes, you can mold the job you already have so that it better fits you.

Moreover, it is what you bring to that job that counts more that the particulars of the job you do. Whether you are a street sweeper, or a yoga teacher, or a lawyer, if you approach each person in your workplace with the underlying intention of spreading wisdom and compassion, you will have a more fulfilling job. And a better work life.

29

The Joy of Voluntary Simplicity

I make myself rich by making my wants few.
—Henry David Thoreau

Want less, suffer less.
—The Buddha

We've already looked at how the active pursuit of pleasure actually creates unhappiness. This is especially true when we try to create happiness by acquiring more and better material things, such as a nicer house, a better car, nicer clothes, and so on and on and on.

But there's another, more subtle aspect to this paradox.

There tends to be an inverse relationship between the amount of things we want and the happiness we enjoy. Put simply, the fewer things we want, the happier we are likely to be. Fewer wants means fewer distractions from living according to our deepest intentions and values.

There's also something to be said for *having* less—for living a life of voluntary simplicity. Of course it makes sense to fulfill your basic needs, and even to enjoy a few luxuries. But once you've reached this point, there are many benefits to stopping or slowing the process of acquisition. You will have fewer things to maintain and watch over, fewer sources of stress, and fewer ways to clutter up your life.

I've practiced voluntary simplicity for years, and it's made my life fuller, not smaller. This is largely because living such a life frees up huge amounts of time. This enables me to fill my life with activities that are meaningful to me—that are aligned with my values—rather than chores associated with maintaining, protecting, or adding to my collection of stuff.

It's a simple equation: fewer things = more time and more freedom.

Another fundamental change also occurs when we practice voluntary simplicity. We realize that the way to happiness is not getting what we want; it is letting go of wanting.

30

Don't Treat the Present Moment Like It's a Shabby Motel Room

We know how to sacrifice ten years for a diploma, or work hard to get a job or a car, but we have difficulty remembering we are alive in the present moment, the only moment there is for us to be alive.
—Thich Nhat Hanh

We live in the now—the present moment. We have nothing else. It is all there is. There is nowhere else we can go and nowhere else we can be.

The past is gone, and we cannot return to it or do it over. The future is not here yet, and there is no way to get to it. What we call the future eventually comes to us—at which point it is not the future, but the present.

Both the past and the future exist only in our imagination. Real life is a series of nows.

Most people don't understand this. As a result, they treat the present moment as if it's a shabby motel room, an unpleasant place they're temporarily stuck in on the way to somewhere more rewarding. They focus their attention on their memories of the past and their fantasies about the future. Meanwhile, they miss the many opportunities to be happy in the only place that is real: the present moment.

We are in the present right now, and we will never be any other place. Life is an incessant stream of moments, all of them taking place now.

I'm not saying that you should just live for the moment and not care about the future. As we've already seen, every one of us needs to plan wisely and be mindful of our goals and intentions. Wise choices made in this moment will help make the moments to come more rewarding.

Nor am I saying that you should ignore the past. Indeed, it's important to examine it, see how it influences you right now, and learn from it. This enables you to change what you think, do, and say in the present.

Here are some common examples of mistreating the present:

I will be happy when... We hear people say this all this time. *I will be happy when I graduate. I will be happy when I get a better job. I will be happy when my partner understands me better.* Each of these messages also implies this one: *I refuse to be happy here and now.*

I made the biggest mistake of my life when... Recognizing poor judgments and learning from them can be very useful. But endlessly replaying them in our mind, and then punishing ourselves for them, hurls us into a mental dungeon, which poisons the present moment.

If only I/he/she/they/it would... Whenever you hear the words *if only*, you know that the speaker has abandoned the present and gotten stuck in their imagination.

We can do many wonderful things in the present moment: observe, play, think, consider, plan, choose, decide, speak, act, experience, and simply be. And the present moment, the here and now, is the *only* place we can ever do them.

Moreover, happiness exists only in the present moment—not in the past, and not in the future. Happiness is only and always now. Our ability to access happiness has more to do with being open and receptive to what life presents to us than it has to do with what we have or will acquire.

Look carefully, and you'll see for yourself that the present moment isn't a shabby motel room at all, but—not always, but often—a penthouse suite with a magnificent view.

31

Attention Matters as Much as Intention

A spiritual warrior sees everything as a challenge, while an ordinary person sees them as a blessing or a curse. For a warrior there are only challenges, which cannot possibly be good or bad, but they are only challenges.

The trick is in what one emphasizes. We either make ourselves miserable, or we make ourselves happy. The amount of work is the same.
—Carlos Castaneda

ife is mysterious.
  Life is precious.
  Life is difficult.
Each statement is true. Life includes all of these facets—sometimes all at once, and sometimes one right after the other.

Our experience of life—and our happiness—depend largely on what we choose to focus on when we face these realities. And what we choose to focus on is largely the result of our intention and attention. They are the keys to the penthouse view.

Intention and attention are two fundamental capacities we all have. These two capacities greatly impact the thoughts that enter our consciousness; the ones that stay there; the ones we choose to act on; and the ones we choose to turn into speech.

They also determine whether we are living in the present, or stuck in a story about the past, or worrying about the future.

As we've seen, we are often ignorant of our intentions. It's easy to act or speak mindlessly, out of habits we've developed (or had ingrained in us). We can spend years, or decades, acting from intentions that have been handed to us by our parents or our culture—or that we chose long ago and haven't questioned or examined since then.

Most people's attention is scattered, not focused. If we don't practice focusing our attention, it can be easily hijacked by whatever bit of trivia floats by—whether our favorite team won, or what a certain movie star is doing, or what someone just wrote on our Facebook page.

As we've also seen, when we learn to focus our attention inward, we can discern the intentions that are operating—and we can change those intentions if we choose. Thus, intention and attention work hand in hand.

Now we're ready to look at some intentions that are especially worth cultivating—and at how to cultivate them.

Using your attention to cultivate wise intentions can change your life.

32

Compassion Can Change Everything

If you want others to be happy, practice compassion. If you want to be happy, practice compassion.

—The Dalai Lama

When people regularly practice playing golf, or riding horses, or growing flowers, they get better at it.

Strangely, though, most of us never think much about practicing anything that can profoundly support our happiness.

Compassion is one of those things.

Compassion often arises naturally, whenever kindness meets pain or suffering. But compassion is also something we can cultivate. Like golf and gardening, the more you practice it, the better you get at it.

It's hard to go wrong if you practice and cultivate compassion. And great things can come of it.

Jack Kornfield tells a wonderful story about the power of compassion, how it is always available to us, and how it can transform people's mental and emotional states.

A man stood in the express lane in a grocery store, holding a carton of milk. He was in a hurry and needed to quickly get through the line, out of the store, and to an important appointment. In front of him was an elderly woman with a baby. The woman had already made her purchases and was chatting with the cashier, a young woman who was admiring the baby. The man waited for the conversation to end, but—to his annoyance and frustration—it didn't. The two women kept talking. Wanting to be polite, and knowing that both women could see him waiting, the man waited silently, while looking periodically at his watch and growing increasingly impatient and angry.

He was just about to say something when the elderly woman handed the baby to the cashier, who held it for a moment while continuing to talk with her customer. The man shook his head, shocked at their lack of consideration.

Finally the cashier handed back the baby, and the elderly woman and baby moved on. The man put his quart of milk in front of the cashier and looked her in the eye, ready to say something disapproving.

The cashier looked back and said, "Thank you so much for waiting. That was my baby and my mom. My husband died recently in the war, and my mother takes care of David while I work. I have to work extra shifts to keep our family going, so mom comes in here a couple of times a day, and that's the only time I see David until nighttime. Thank you for waiting a moment while I held my baby."

There are many profound things about this story, but there are two that I'd like to highlight.

First, while the man waited in line, he chose to get angry and frustrated. But those emotions disappeared when compassion arose in him. His external circumstances didn't change at all—but when the cashier told him about her family, his attitude toward his situation completely transformed. So did yours, probably, as you listened to the story.

This story also highlights the power of compassion to change our intentions, beliefs, and actions. We've already seen that, while you cannot control your thoughts, you can choose which ones to give energy to, and which ones to release. Compassion helps us let go of blame, resentment, or revenge, freeing us from much unnecessary suffering. With practice, over time, compassion will even have an influence on how often our various thoughts and mental stories show up.

When practicing compassion, it's important to include compassion for yourself. Having compassion for yourself can help you let go of mental stories about what a victim you are, or how unlucky you are, or how someone else hates or disrespects you.

In short, cultivating compassion—for others and for yourself—is a great way to cultivate your own happiness. Indeed, it's a key to freedom. No matter what happens, it will help you to accept and live through life's difficulties without undue pain or suffering.

33

Help Yourself by Forgiving Others

Not forgiving is like drinking rat poison and then waiting for
the rat to die.
—Anne Lamott

The weak can never forgive. Forgiveness is the attribute
of the strong.
—Mohandas Gandhi

used to think forgiveness was something you do for someone else—
something you do to help them.

I had it largely backward.

Forgiving someone else takes place inside *you*. And, whatever
good it may do for others, it also greatly improves *your own* mental
state.

The healing force of forgiveness creates peace—not just between people, but in your own mind and heart. As a result, it also encourages better decision making and more long-term happiness.

Better still—as with golfing, gardening, and compassion—your capacity to forgive can be deliberately developed.

Imagine that someone close to you—your sister, let's say—borrows your iPhone. She absent-mindedly leaves it in a coffee shop, where it's quickly stolen. But she refuses to apologize or pay for it. "People lose their cell phones all the time," she says. "Get over it. There's an Apple store seven blocks away."

So you get angry. It's so obvious that you're being reasonable and she's acting childish. You're slightly angry that she was thoughtless and careless, but you're outraged that she won't take responsibility for what happened. You decide that until she says she's sorry, you're going to be mad at her and treat her disrespectfully.

Where does all this get you? Are you happier? Are you making your sister happier? Are you making anyone else—the friends you complain to about your sister, for example—any happier? Are you making your relationship with your sister better or worse?

You're entirely justified in feeling that your sister was careless, unreasonable, and unfair. You're equally justified in not loaning her your new cell phone—or, perhaps, anything else—for as long as she continues to act irresponsibly.

But forgiveness is another matter entirely.

Forgiveness has a profound effect on *your own* mental state. For as long as you refuse to forgive your sister—and for as long as you cling to your anger—you make yourself less happy.

Forgiving someone doesn't mean you condone or forget their actions. Nor does it mean that you don't take what they did into account when dealing with them in the future. You may need to set stronger, clearer boundaries with them. You may need to say "no" (or even "hell, no!") to them often. In certain cases, you may even need to end the relationship.

But you can also forgive them—for your own benefit as well as theirs.

Forgiveness promotes peace of mind and reduces anger and resentment. It allows you to deal with situations more realistically, so you can bring greater wisdom to them.

Forgiving your sister has nothing to do with making up with her, or even with determining who is right. It has to do choosing peace and equanimity over anger and agitation. It is a way to be more compassionate with yourself.

And what does forgiveness cost you? Nothing.

Forgiveness becomes even more important to your happiness when the person you forgive is yourself. Self-blame—and its darker cousin, self-loathing—can be deeply painful mental states, and many people suffer from them.

When we refuse to forgive ourselves, it's easy to get caught in a loop—or a downward spiral—of suffering. As a result, forgiving yourself for your own past conduct is often the first and most important step in changing your life for the better.

Forgiving yourself does not mean forgetting or condoning what you did, or avoiding any responsibilities, consequences, or amends. It simply means that you release yourself from the bondage of unnecessary suffering, so that you can make positive changes and wiser choices in the future.

Forgiving others adds to your happiness. Forgiving yourself also adds to your happiness. How great is that?

34

Want What You Have—Not What You Don't Have

All the time you go around wanting what you don't have and not wanting what you do have. You should just reverse it. Why not want what you have and not want what you don't have?
—Nisargadatta Maharaj

Most of us suffer not from a lack of things, but from a *sense* that we lack things.

It is not the lack of a particular thing that brings us unhappiness. Rather, it is our *attachment* to the things we don't have that causes much of our suffering.

Most Americans are among the luckiest people to ever live on Earth. Historically speaking, we live in a time and in a land of great prosperity and peace. Most of us don't have to wonder where our next meal will come from. We don't live in the midst of war, where our primary goal each day is simply to stay alive. We don't spend the winter shivering and trying to keep warm.

If we are at all objective about it, most of us will realize that we live better than 95%—in many cases, 99%—of the world's population. Yet, somehow, we *feel* otherwise. In fact, sometimes the people with the most things most tend to feel that they *lack* things. That's because we often focus on what we lack, or on what others have that we don't, or on what we hope to acquire someday that we don't have now, rather than on appreciating what we've got.

None of this supports our happiness.

And none of it is true.

Focusing on what we lack renders invisible many of the good things we already have. It also makes it harder for us to notice when something new and good comes across our path. It's a kind of blindness that limits our view of the world.

We all know that peace and happiness come from security. But most of us believe that security comes from getting the things we desire and then hanging onto them. Or from turning the world into just what we want it to be. Or from making *ourselves* into just what we want to be—by getting the right job, or wearing the right clothes, or marrying the right person, or getting plastic surgery and liposuction, etc.

But none of those things makes us secure—rather they breed *insecurity,* as we know deep down we can't always win the "getting and keeping" game.

There is, however, another way—one that genuinely *does* create security and support our peace and happiness. It's the security of knowing that an acquisition-oriented approach to life inevitably leads to fear and anxiety. It's the security of understanding that we won't always get what we want. It's the security of openness, of awareness, of being comfortable with knowing that life is uncertain. It's the security of focusing on being present and aware instead of on acquiring, keeping, and protecting.

With this security as our foundation, we can enjoy and share what we have—and we can be thankful for it.

If we each spent just a few minutes a day being grateful for what we have, most of us would discover that we already have what we need. We'd also realize that it's impossible to feel grateful and impoverished at the same time. And we might also discover equanimity and, yes, even happiness.

I already mentioned one simple, quick way to grow gratitude in an earlier chapter—the practice of each day writing down the 10 things you are most grateful for, and why. If you haven't tried it yet, give it a try now, and for the next week. I really do mean to write them down—slowly, mindfully, and in longhand.

You'll quickly discover that if you do this regularly, it will completely reorient your approach to life. Over time, it will change how you see the world and the attitude you bring to life's events. As your perspective changes, so too will your experience of life, without changing life's external events at all.

35

Be Selfish—Give Generously

Generosity brings happiness at every stage of its expression.
We experience joy in forming the intention to be generous. We
experience joy in the actual act of giving something. And we
experience joy in remembering the fact that we have given.
—Buddha

We live in a balance-sheet culture. Most of us keep track of what we have given—and what we believe we should get back. Generosity feels like a luxury, perhaps one we can't afford. As a result, many of us measure and manage and ration our generosity.

But generosity isn't about how much, or what, we give. It's about the spirit in which we give.

Generosity involves giving freely—of your time, your money, your resources, and your attention. *Giving freely* doesn't mean giving everything, or giving so much that you harm yourself or your family.

It means giving whole-heartedly, without conditions, and without expecting anything back.

This naturally creates freedom. In fact, you'll eventually discover that generosity, like forgiveness and compassion, benefits you as much as it does the people who receive it. It can transform anger, fear, dread, and other painful mind states into equanimity and joy.

One of the most generous things you can do is give others your full attention and presence. This is especially true with your partner and kids, who value your presence and attention more than anything.

The ultimate act of generosity is to treat every person you encounter with lovingkindness.

36
Lovingkindness is the Ultimate Reset Button

The difference between misery and happiness depends on what we do with our attention.
—Sharon Salzberg

This is my simple religion. There is no need for temples; no need for complicated philosophy. Our own brain, our own heart is our temple; the philosophy is kindness.
—The Dalai Lama

Lovingkindness is wishing for the happiness and well-being of everyone—others *and* yourself.

Compassion, forgiveness, generosity, and gratitude all have lovingkindness at their core. So do many other beneficial states of mind, such as patience, equanimity, and joy.

Our capacity for lovingkindness is innate. We are all born with it. But our culture promotes some beliefs that cover up that capacity. We're taught that it's more important to get what we want (materially and otherwise) than to wish others (and ourselves) well. This is why so many people sacrifice their health and sanity to make more money so they can get a bigger house, a better car, a more attractive partner, etc. It's also why many people choose to spend far more time working than with their loved ones. And it's why people approach so much of what they do with anxiety, fear, greed, or anger.

Lovingkindness is a much more solid, healthy, and lasting approach to life. Mindfully selecting what we are going to do, and then doing it with lovingkindness, naturally leads to far more happiness—both for ourselves and for the people whose lives we touch.

So it is worth spending some time cultivating lovingkindness. Here's a very simple way to do it:

Each day, spend a few minutes wishing the following:

First, wish that you will be happy, safe, healthy, and at peace. (This doesn't mean wishing for particular things, situations, or outcomes that you think will "make" you happy, safe, healthy, and at peace. Instead, wish for your happiness, safety, health, and peace *no matter what happens*.)

Next, wish these same four things for the people close to you.

Then wish these things for everyone else you may come into contact with.

Lastly, wish these things for all the people you have difficulty with: your angry ex-partner, your overbearing boss, your disrespectful roommate, the pickpocket who took your wallet, the people in the political party you most disagree with, etc. Wish for the happiness, safety, health, and peace of everyone you consider the "other" or the enemy.

Interestingly, you don't have to feel loving, or generous, or compassionate, to cultivate and practice lovingkindness. Sometimes you might even feel exactly the opposite. That's all right. Let yourself feel what you feel. Simply wish people well.

This practice is about changing your focus and intentions, not your feelings or behavior. But, as you will see, over time your feelings and actions—toward others and toward yourself—*will* change in a positive and wonderful way.

Earlier in this book, when we looked at meditation, it involved paying attention to your breath and releasing your thoughts. These lovingkindness practices are also a form of meditation, in which you repeat these wishes to yourself as you breathe. (The book *Real Happiness* by Sharon Salzberg offers a more detailed description and discussion of lovingkindness meditation—and other forms of meditation as well.)

In Chapter 21, I wrote about a reset button that you can use when you feel hopeless or angry or afraid. Lovingkindness is another reset button. And it can work for anyone, in relation to anyone, in almost any situation.

Best of all, lovingkindness is a capacity you already have.

37

The Art of Living is the Art of Starting Over

The important thing is this: to at any moment be able to sacrifice what we are for what we could become.
—Charles Dubois

Happiness is an art—and, like other arts, it requires practice and effort.

Our happiness depends, in part, on our being able to start over when we find ourselves caught or stuck. This usually means letting go of harmful mental states or patterns, and taking up something more skillful and beneficial. Often this involves dropping habits like anger and hopelessness and developing certain qualities we already have, such as gratitude, compassion, forgiveness, and generosity.

These efforts do more than just bring us happiness; they also help us weather the storms of unwanted and unexpected events.

The term *let go* is widely used, and perhaps overused. Yet, properly understood, it may be the single most important key to our happiness.

The obvious question is, *let go of what?* Depending on your situation, you might let go of particular ideas, beliefs, practices, habits, attachments, hopes, demands, expectations, relationships, strategies, and inner stories that don't serve you (or others) well.

Letting go does *not* mean letting go of your drive to live fully, to be present and engaged with the world. It doesn't mean becoming a passive recipient of whatever comes to you in life. That's not letting go; that's apathy.

Sometimes we need to fight for what is genuinely important in life—things such as freedom, equality, safety, fairness, and respect. Letting go doesn't mean dropping, or even lessening, the vigor with which we pursue these important values. In fact, some of the world's experts at letting go are also known as warriors for humanity. Look at Gandhi, Aung San Suu Kyi, Mother Teresa, Nelson Mandela, and the Dalai Lama. Study their lives and you'll see that their ability to act courageously, often in the face of danger and difficulty, was directly related to their ability to let go and begin again.

These people teach us that when we let go of the things that don't serve us, we become better able to make good decisions and take wise action. Having let go of despair, frustration, anger, or an unhelpful pattern of thought or action, we are free to improve the situation, often in a unique or unexpected way.

Every act of letting go has both an *of* and an *into* aspect. When, for example, we let go *of* an old habit or cherished idea, this allows us to move *into* a new way of seeing, understanding, or working with the situation. We let go of fear and into courage. We let go of greed and into gratitude. We let go of blame and into cooperation. We drop something that's unhelpful and replace it with something better.

When the question facing us is *What do I do now?*, letting go is often the answer—or, at least, part of the answer. Let go of the story that you are a failure. Let go of the habit of playing video games to avoid grieving the end of a relationship. Let go of the habit of reliving painful memories. Let go of the notion that you are entitled to a perfect life. Let go of the hope that you will change your partner. Let go of the expectation that you can (or ought to) perfectly control your subordinates, or your kids, or your cat. Let go of the assumption that life can be what you want it to be, if only you do everything perfectly.

Let go into something new and different—perhaps into generosity or gratitude or lovingkindess.

Sacrifice what you are—or think you are—for what you can become.

38

Living Happily Takes Practice

Tune the instrument and let it play.
—Charlie Parker

Our instrument for living is our combined mind and body. Once we tune this instrument properly, all we need to do is let it play.

The process of tuning involves training the mind to let go, to pay attention, and to select the most skillful intentions and actions, especially in difficult situations.

This book is meant to answer the question: *How can I train my attention—tune my bodymind—to promote happiness for myself and others?*

As we've seen, the process of tuning goes by the names *awareness* or *mindfulness* or *meditation* (or, sometimes, *mindfulness meditation*). This process is at once down-to-earth and transformative, and both very simple and (for some people) difficult at first.

As you've seen, the primary activity of meditation is paying attention to your breath. You don't try to control the breath; you just let it happen naturally. As thoughts and images and impulses arise—and they will—don't try to hang onto them or push them away. Let them come and let them go.

As necessary, gently remind yourself not to follow—or be captured by—either the thoughts that arise or the events that happen around you. When your minds strays, simply return to the breath, and let the thoughts pass through.

Do this every day for 20 minutes. Over time, you will come to love your breath. You will come to love yourself. And you will come to love others.

While you sit silently, you can also learn to practice compassion, patience, forgiveness, gratitude, lovingkindness, and all the other practices that promote a happy life.

Sometimes your mind will be very unruly. This is 100% normal, and nothing to worry about or be ashamed of. These periods of unruliness are opportunities to develop your compassion, patience, forgiveness, gratitude, lovingkindness, etc. (If you're like me and almost everyone else on the planet, you'll have many such opportunities.)

In practicing mindfulness meditation, you simply pay attention, moment after moment, without reacting or judging. You give full but nonjudgmental attention to whatever arises—inside or outside of you—with an open heart. You note your direct experience—the sounds around you, the sensations in your body, your emotions, your impulses, your thoughts—as well as the things you add to that experience, such as inner stories, projections, hopes, fears, and expectations. But you don't allow yourself to get wrapped up in those thoughts or stories—because you are constantly returning to your primary focus of attention, your breath.

Here's what usually happens to people during the first few times they practice mindfulness meditation:

Within a few seconds, thoughts pop into your head. These thoughts soon hijack your attention, taking it away from your breath, just as they do during day-to-day life. After a while, you notice this and bring your attention back to your breath.

Soon you realize you're running down a different rabbit trail with a different random thought. So, once again, you gently refocus your attention on your breath.

This happens over and over and over. Each time you notice that you've run away with a thought, you calmly and gently—with understanding and compassion—turn your attention back to your breath.

You will quickly notice that your mind is like a carnival midway, with all kinds of thoughts popping up and capturing your attention. This is normal.

Your job is to just breathe and notice. Don't get wrapped up in any one thought. As necessary, bring your attention back to your breath, like you would gently bring a puppy back to the spot where you want it to sit and stay.

How does this help you live a sane and happy life?

First, you cultivate an ability to see what your actual experience is, and what extras—stories, projections, expectations, assumptions, etc.—you add to it. With practice, you can begin to discern which, if any, of these add-ons are accurate. (For most people, almost none of them are.) Then, when a false story or assumption arises, you can simply note its appearance—and its falseness—and let it drift off.

Second, meditation develops the capacity to choose where to place your attention. Instead of letting it be hijacked by whatever comes along, you can deliberately and mindfully move it to the activities and thoughts you value most.

Third, it helps you choose—and return to—your intention. When you meditate, your intention is to follow your breath. However, this practice helps you strengthen your ability to stay with *any* intention. If your intention is to be grateful, or compassionate, or generous, or forgiving, through meditation you grow your ability to maintain (or quickly return to) that intention.

Fourth, mindfulness meditation helps you cultivate the art of beginning again. When you focus on your breath, each new in-breath is a new beginning, and each out-breath is an opportunity to release all that your mind has been holding. Each time you lose your way and realize that you've followed a thought down a rabbit trail, you have the chance to bring your mind back to your breath. Meditation thus helps you take a fresh perspective on each moment of your life.

In all these respects, meditation is the art of starting over, again and again and again. It's the perfect practice for life.

39

Your Body is Your Pathway to the Present— and Your Vehicle to Your Future

To keep the body in good health is a duty....Otherwise we shall not be able to keep our mind strong and clear.
—Buddha

Treat your body as if it's your own.
—Jake Roberson, yoga instructor

Your body is a great place to practice awareness. If you pay attention, your body can tell you all you need to know about how you're showing up right now. But you have to listen to it. Most of the time, most people don't.

Your body will tell you if you are stressed, angry, sad, happy, depressed, or buoyant. It is always in the present. In fact, your body is your most reliable source of information about how you are responding to external and internal events. If you quiet your mind and pay attention, your body will provide you with many subtle (and, sometimes, not-so-subtle) signals. When I'm angry, my body tenses up all over. When I'm afraid, I feel an adrenaline rush, especially up and down my arms. When I am anxious, I feel tension in my shoulders and neck. When I am relaxed, my body has an ease and calm to it. Thus your body can be a wonderful anchor to the present.

But it also can be a great vehicle into the future. That is, if we treat our body well, it will be able to propel us into the future with great energy and vigor.

Unfortunately, many of us treat our bodies shabbily, like unimportant possessions. We give our bodies too much of things that are not good for them, and too little of the things they need. We would never treat our pets, or even our cars, with such disdain and neglect.

The book *Savor* by Thich Nhat Hanh offers a wonderful antidote. It explores how we can change our habits—and increase our happiness—through mindful awareness at each meal, and through exercise and movement. It helps us see that each meal—and each movement, and each moment—is an opportunity for the mindful appreciation of life.

Most people in our culture don't use our bodies in the ways or to the extent they were intended. Many of us work too much; many of us sit around too much; some of us do both.

The human body was made to move—to walk, to lift things, to climb, to crawl, to jump, to stretch, to be active. It was designed to sit for only an hour or two at a time. (That's why, if you have a desk job, your butt or your back hurts by the end of the day.) Show compassion for your body and yourself by providing it with the exercise it needs and deserves.

Moving or using your body is an ideal way to bring yourself into the present. When you are hiking a trail, running up or down a hill, shooting a basket, riding a horse, or stretching and holding a yoga pose, you have the opportunity to be totally present. Fully inhabiting your body, you can practice attention, compassion, mindfulness, and wise intention.

Your body is a prime example of cause and effect. Treat it well and pay proper attention to it, and it will repay that attention many times over. Treat it badly and you (and it) will suffer.

Your body is also the perfect vehicle for exploring and appreciating precious moments—and for realizing that, in fact, every moment is precious.

40

Your Happiness is in Your Hands

> *Everything has its wonders, even darkness and silence, and I learn, whatever state I may be in, therein to be content.*
> —Helen Keller

> *The purpose of our lives is to be happy.*
> —The Dalai Lama

n every moment of your life, you get to choose. You can make choices that point in the direction of long-term happiness—or you can make choices that point elsewhere. And in each new moment, you get to choose anew.

Human beings all want to be happy. The desire for happiness is innate, like breathing. But our culture, and other influences, do not promote a path to real happiness. That's why this book has been about making choices that promote your (and others') genuine happiness.

As we've seen, this is not the same as short-term pleasure, which most people mistake for happiness.

Instead I propose here a different approach, involving looking inside yourself, and making choices. What attitude will you choose? What goals will you pursue? What intentions will you select? What will you do and say? Are your actions and speech aligned with your goals and intentions?

If you make your choices skillfully, then your happiness will not be determined solely—or at all—by what happens to you.

The truth is that we have no idea what all the positive and negative ramifications of any event will be.

You cannot control all (or, sometimes, any) of the events that play out in your life. Nor can you fully determine (or, at times, even see) where life will take you. But in every moment you can pay close and careful attention, and wisely choose your intentions. You can meet each moment with wisdom, compassion, generosity, and lovingkindness.

You will learn—if you haven't learned already—that your happiness doesn't depend on where you choose to go, or how fast you get there, or whether you get there at all. Instead, it depends on how you meet each moment.

You will also discover that it is possible to be at peace—and, sometimes, even happy—in very difficult situations.

The things that happen to you will never be fully in your control. But your peace in the face of those events *is* something you can choose to cultivate.

Staying present, letting go, and living a life aligned with your values and intentions are not always easy. Often they require effort. But they also create balance, equanimity, and wisdom—and they promote long-term happiness.

I hope these chapters have provided some wisdom and encouragement about what choices to make.

Now it's up to you.

Acknowledgments

want to gratefully acknowledge my editor, consigliere, and advisor Scott Edelstein. His editing—and, even more importantly, his insights—helped to transform a series of e-mails written over a few years into a book. And his continued advice helped turn a wayward manuscript into a published work. It would never have turned out this way without his help.

I want to thank my good friends Larry Tannenbaum and Rod Betts, who in our runs (and now, in our advancing years, hikes) listened to hours of my musings. Their ideas contributed to many of the chapters here. Each of you will know exactly where some of this stuff came from. Thanks for listening and contributing.

I want to also acknowledge the Morgan James family: David Hancock, Megan Malone, and all the others who contributed to publishing this book. David, you took a chance on a rookie, and you and your team could not have been more helpful, respectful, professional, and collegial. It was a truly rewarding experience for which I am deeply grateful.

About the Author

John **Allcock** has succeeded big time, many times. He's also failed big time, many times. Ultimately, what seemed like some of the worst things in his life were what began to wake him up. Those failures and difficulties helped him realize something important: although he, like all human beings, sought happiness, he actually was looking in exactly the wrong direction.

John graduated from Boston College (with highest honors in philosophy and political science) and Harvard Law School (cum laude). He works as a trial lawyer at DLA Piper, where he is also the Global Co-Chair of the firm's Intellectual Property Group and serves on the firm's Executive Committee.

He is a longtime student of Jack Kornfield, Gil Fronsdal, Thich Nhat Hahn, and other meditation teachers. He and his wife Cheryl have developed a curriculum in mindfulness for schools that has been implemented at Sea Change Preparatory, a small school they founded in Del Mar, California.

John lives in San Diego, where his regular activities include yoga, meditation, hiking, open ocean swimming, and simply breathing and being.

He is the father of three grown daughters (who inspired this book), as well as a grown stepson.